T0128395

International Journal of Security and Strategic Studies

MAIDEN EDITION

IJoSSS

WESTBOW
PRESS®
A DIVISION OF THOMAS NELSON
& ZONDERVAN

Editorial Note

This is the first edition of International Journal of Security and Strategic Studies (IJoSSS). The journal seeks to promote quality, contemporary, and dynamic researches in diverse fields of endeavor.

IJoSSS presents national, regional and international perspectives on Security, Human security strategy issues and studies from historical and reality assessments. By disseminating professional, graduate research and all-purpose research work internationally, IJoSSS seeks to facilitate students, scholars and professional acquisition of knowledge from alternative viewpoints allowing them to further develop critical thinking, problem-solving, and global competencies required to lead in a complex world.

The goal of this publication notwithstanding, all expressions, views, citations and presentations in papers published in this journal does not represent the policies and views of the authoring organisation. The accuracy of facts and figures presented in articles of the journal and therefore cannot be responsible for any error in such articles.

Prof. O. Akinwumi PhD, AvHF, FHCN
Editor in Chief

WestBow Press books may be ordered through booksellers or by contacting:

WestBow Press
A Division of Thomas Nelson & Zondervan
1663 Liberty Drive
Bloomington, IN 47403
www.westbowpress.com
1 (866) 928-1240

ISBN: 978-1-9736-7789-5 (sc)
ISBN: 978-1-9736-7788-8 (e)

Print information available on the last page.

WestBow Press rev. date: 12/18/2019

A Critical Investigation into the Role of Security Sector Agencies in the Jos Conflict: Issues and Strategies for Institutional/Security Sector Reform.

Oluwafunmilayo J Para-Mallam, mni
Professor, Gender and Development
Directing Staff (Special Duties), Directorate of Studies,
National Institute for Policy & Strategic Studies,
Kuru-Nigeria.
Email: layo_le@yahoo.co.uk
Tel: +2348036343793

Kate Hoomlong, PhD
Centre for Conflict Management
and Peace Studies,
University of Jos,
Jos-Nigeria
Email:
Tel:

Abstract

The study investigated the roles played by security agencies, specifically the Special Task Force, in carrying out the mandate to restore law and order in the wake of violent ethno-religious conflict in Jos since 2010. The study employed a combined quantitative and qualitative research strategy to explore the perspectives of residents in five local government areas considered as the epicentre of violence. The LGAs selected were Barkin Ladi, Jos East, Jos North, Jos South and Riyom. Security sector reform theory provided the theoretical frame of analysis albeit with suggest modifications to suit the peculiarities of Nigerian socio-political contexts. Findings from the research underscore critical areas requiring security sector reform including institutional capacity building for the Nigeria Police Force, and effective grievance and complaints channels accessible to citizens to ensure accountability on the part of security agents.

Key Words: Security sector reform, democratic governance, ethnoreligious crisis/conflict, conflict management/ transformation, peacebuilding

Introduction and Background to the Study

The overall aim of this research is to examine the roles played by security sector agencies in the perennial violent conflict in Jos, the Plateau State capital, and its environs. More specifically, the study considers of the role of the Special Task Force in responding to violent conflict and post-conflict situations in Jos East, Jos North, Jos South, Barkin Ladi and Riyoml LGAs since January 2010 (see map showing research sites in Fig. 1). These locations remain the epicentre of hostilities, with some seeing greater continuation of violence than others. The wider scope and higher intensity of the Jos conflict since 2010 merits an investigation into the unique characteristics and dynamics of conflict management since that time. Indeed, the twin calls for state actors to demonstrate political will to address the roots and results of ethno-religious violence and to initiate security sector reform have become a recurrent decimal in the public discourse on Nigerian security issues (Gofwen, 2011; Ambe-Uva, 2006). Empirical research findings are required to give impetus to the much-needed government policy decisions and actions that would feed into wide-ranging security sector reform towards achieving de facto peace and security. This is the essence of the study. A previous study by Best and Hoomlong (2011) highlights a number of gaps in existing literature as critical focal points vital for future research. Chief among these is the absence of an analysis of security sector engagement and management, particularly with regard to the role and rules of engagement of security apparatuses during violent conflict. Unpacking the various roles of these agencies is essential to understanding the nature and dynamics of conflict transformation processes, notably how conflict situations escalate, degenerate into violence and are resolved, albeit temporarily. More importantly, it would provide insight into conceptual, structural and methodological gaps in conflict management within the present pattern of conflict response in the country. Para-Mallam (2011) suggests that failure to institute SSR contributes to the weak the institutional capability to manage conflict in Plateau state and in Nigeria. As such governments at all levels are under such a crisis of credibility and confidence to the extent of undermining the legitimacy of governance altogether.

Why, despite the declaration of a state of emergency in the five LGAs under study, and the presence of security personnel in those areas, do violent attacks continue? Is it merely due to operational lapses or can allegations of complicity in violence be supported with concrete evidence? What are the dimensions, dynamics and implications of the alleged complicity of various key state and non-state actors in the Jos conflict? What structural and practical strategies can governments devise to mitigate the negative effects of such engagements in the immediate and long-term? These questions are at the core of the research problem.

The Research Context

Historical Antecedents to the Jos Conflict Plateau State occupies 26,899 square kilometres of Nigerian territory and lies between latitude 80°24'N and longitude 80°32' and 100°38' east in the North Central geopolitical zone (See map in Fig. 1). It has a population of 3.5 million people (2006 Census). The location and unique temperate climate of Nigeria earned it the epithet "Home of Peace and Tourism." This reputation has been seriously ruptured since violent outbreaks began in 2001.

Ethno-religious violence in Jos, Plateau State is a concrete example of deep-rooted identity-based conflict arising from structural defects in the Nigeria's dysfunctional system of citizenship rights. At the core of this conflict lie the ambiguities and inconsistencies that characterise the indigene/settler divide and the differential entitlements and rights that accrue to citizens depending on which part of the country they reside (Best, 2001; Adetula, 2005; Alubo, 2008; Egwu, 2009). This is complicated by two factors: first is the tension between protecting cultural/religious identity and heritage (particularly, but not exclusively of indigenous minorities) on the one hand, and promoting national integration as reflected in the constitutionally enshrined Federal Character principle on the other. The second factor is the historical (pre-colonial) antecedent of Hausa-Fulani cultural, religious and political dominance in northern Nigeria (Goshit, 2006; Adam, 2010). Against this backdrop, the indigenous ethnic minority groups making up Plateau state in the north central geopolitical zone have a space for the assertion of their cultural identity and political administration within the Nigerian Federation. These indigenous minority groups are historically recorded to have, somewhat successfully, resisted Islamic incursions since the 19th Century Uthman Dan Fodio Jihad (Plateau Indigenous Development Association of Nigeria (PIDAN), 2010). They constitute a conspicuous tapestry of predominantly Christians and a minority of animists and indigenous Muslims. There is also a sizeable 'settler' population comprising southerners (predominantly Christians) and Hausa-Fulani Muslims, many of whose parents, or they themselves, were born and raised in Plateau and consider it their home. However, the ethno-religious configuration of Plateau has turned the Hausa-Fulani, a majority ethno-religious group in Nigeria, into a minority group within a majority Christian state. Sporadic episodes of tension, between Hausa-Fulani Muslims and indigenous Christians, began in pre-colonial times and persisted through colonial and post-colonial times without escalating to the level of violence (Potnicov, 1970). For historical and political reasons, inter-ethnic tensions and conflicts have also plagued relations among indigenous groups around Jos – the Anaguta, Afizere and Berom. However, until recently, the various settler and indigenous groups were able to maintain a climate of peaceful socioeconomic co-existence. Latent frictions boiled over in 1994 as an aftermath of the creation of Jos North Local Government Area by the Babangida-led military administration (Sha, 1998). The move was perceived by the indigenous population as a political strategy towards the takeover of Jos by the Hausa-Fulani whose population and economic and political influence were on the increase (Best, 2007). For their part, the Hausa-Fulani population have often laid allegations of collective marginalization against successive Plateau state governments, specifically in relation to the denial of indigene rights and privileges (Blench and Dendo, 2003; Ostein, 2009). In rebuttal to this assertion, Plateau state governments point to a number of well-placed Muslims of Hausa-Fulani decent who have represented the state in federal appointed and elective posts. Mutually destructive discourses of Islamist agendas and ethnoreligious marginalization eventually erupted in open hostilities. The cycle of ethno-religious violence widened to include Christians and Muslims from other parts of the country resident in Jos and culminated in massive outbreaks that gained increasing momentum since 2001, 2004, 2008 and 2010 in various parts of the state, especially Jos the state capital, and surrounding areas.

Selected Episodes of Violence and Time Line of Events (2010–2012) In order to buttress the repeated and protracted nature of violence in Plateau State, notwithstanding the presence of the Special Task Force, we have selected the following episodes to buttress the point. These also illustrate the need to understand the operations of the STF in a more coherent manner, in the context of human security and the state.

- January 17 2010 - Hundreds are reported killed after clashes between Muslim and Christian gangs in Jos, most by gunfire. Police estimate death toll at 326, although some community leaders put the figure at more than 400.
- Jan 22, 2010- 150 bodies allegedly confirmed dead and pulled from a well in Kuru Karama
- March 2010 - Hundreds of people are killed in clashes between Islamic pastoralists and Christian villagers in the mostly Christian villages of Dogo Nahawa, Zot and Ratsat just south of Jos. Plateau State Commissioner for Information Gregory Yenlong said more than 300 people had died.
- December 2010 - At least 80 people are killed in Dec. 24 bombings as well as in clashes two days later between Muslim and Christian youths in Jos.
- January 2011 - Human Rights Watch says more than 200 people killed in violence over preceding month, many hacked to death or burned alive in attacks on villages, and reprisal killings in Plateau state.
- July 20 2011- 5 people killed in fresh violence between Christian and Muslim youths in Angwan Rukuba.
- August-September 2011 - At least 70 people killed in clashes in central Plateau state. Violence started when Christian youths attacked Muslims gathering to celebrate end of Ramadan in Jos.
- October 6 2011 unknown assailants attacked Gwol village in Barkin Ladi, injuring nine and killing one
- September 11, 2011 2 explosive devices were thrown at the West of Mines area and a number of casualties were injured.
- September 2011- attacks in 2 villages of Barkin Ladi; kakpwis in Foron district and Kuzen of Gashit district.
- February 2012 suicide bombers attack at COCIN Headquarters and St Finbarrs Catholic Church, Rayfield.
- July 8 2012. 14 rural communities were attacked, namely Gashish, Matse village 63 people killed, Barkin Ladi incessant attacks levelled on the villages by marauding Fulani militias. A total of 103 people killed including senator Dantong and Hon. Danfulani.
- November 19 2012 retaliatory killings July 29 2012 bloody attacks and killings of over a hundred people from the Berom extraction in Riyom and Barkin Ladi LGAs led to the STF at the prompting of the presidency to root out the suspected mercenaries hiding in the villages of Mahanga, Kakuruk, Kuzen, Maseh and Shong and terrorizing the communities.
- August and September 2012 had human loses of 180 victims and attendant silent killings.
- October 11 2012 suspected Fulani herdsmen killed 14 people in three villages in Riyom LGA against Fulani's in Bachit village.
- November 26 2012. The gruesome killing of eight people at a beer parlour in Heipang, Barkin Ladi by men dressed in military fatigues in a Toyota Hilux van belonging to the Special Task Force.

Conflict Escalation and Security Sector Intervention Since 2010

On 17th January 2010 violence erupted in Jos; it spread and engulfed broad segments of the indigenous and settler population on a scale that was more destructive and pervasive than any previous crisis. Most importantly, the meddling influences of extraneous forces such as neighbouring state governments, mercenaries and political factions assumed huge proportions.

This is highlighted by a resolution passed by the Bauchi State House of Assembly in May 2010 to expel Plateau indigenes resident in Bauchi and also to vote in favour of a proposal for the dismemberment of Plateau state. Such political manoeuvres and the presence of mercenaries significantly heightened tensions and animosities among the various ethno-religious groups, inciting more violence. It soon became apparent that the situation was beyond the capacity of the illequipped Nigeria Police Force to contain. In fact, the then Police Commissioner, Mr Gregory Anyanting was re-deployed with despatch for releasing a Press Statement alleging that initial police investigations indicated that a group of Hausa Muslim youth had initiated the violence (CMG, 2010). The escalation of the conflict within and around Jos prompted the Federal Government to resort to military intervention. Internal security operations carried out to suppress insurrection are supported by Section 217 subsection 2(c) of the 1999 Constitution of the Federal Republic of Nigeria. The provision allows for the military to act in aid of the civil authority in the maintenance of public order and internal security where the situation demands, subject to such conditions as prescribed by an act of the National Assembly. The initial deployment of soldiers to bring the violence under control alongside the declaration of a 24-hour curfew initially stemmed the tide of violence. However, the initial containment soon gave way to allegations of ethno-religious bias in military conduct and silent killings motivated by ethno-religious sentiments persisted at various flashpoints around Jos and environs.

Since March 2010, a Special Joint Military Task Force (STF) has been permanently stationed in Jos and its environs to ensure that underlying animosity resulting from perennial ethno-religious hostilities do not erupt into a fresh round of violence (Newswatch, 2010). By 2011, what initially appeared largely to be a 'Jos problem' assumed wider ramifications highlighted through the meddling influences referred to earlier and the insurgency of Boko Haram (an Islamist terrorist group originating in Borno state). The group increased the rate and scope of violent attacks against state institutions and symbols after the April 2011 elections, which installed Mr Goodluck Jonathan as President. In addition, the Boko Haram made it clear that it had an anti-establishment, anti-Christian and pro-fundamentalist Islamist agenda. Security personnel, particularly police officers and stations, public offices and Muslims perceived to be in alliance with the 'western secular' state were attacked and eliminated. The Sect also moved to expunge Christian presence from northern Nigeria. On 1st January, 2012 it issued a seven-day ultimatum demanding that all Christians, whether they were indigenes or settlers, leave northern Nigeria or face extermination. The sect spokesman also declared the intention to launch violent attacks within Jos in retaliation for the killing of Muslims during the previous violent crisis. Thus, the initiation of bomb blasts by the sect in and around Christian dominated areas in Jos, including church premises, in December 2010, April 2011, February, March and June 2012 added a new twist to the conflict. In December 2011, spiralling Boko Haram insurgency in Borno, Yobe, Bauchi, Gombe and Kano states, as well as continued ethno-religious violence in the

Jos area, led the federal government to declare a state of emergency in various local government areas across those states. In Plateau state this included the five LGAs under study.

Yet, despite the continued presence of the STF in these locations Fulani herdsmen persist in raiding Berom farmlands and killing and displacing the local populace. The Fulani accuse the local Berom population of rustling their cattle, and some Fulani have also been killed. Intermittent bomb blasts in churches, for which the Boko Haram were quick to claim responsibility, continued to claim lives, damage property and create a climate of insecurity. In addition, 'faceless' gunmen began inflicting brutal attacks on locals in Riyom and Barkin Ladi LGAs at local pubs, on farm routes and farmlands and even in their homes. Consequently, calls for the recall of the STF from different segments of the population, including open protest marches by women dressed in black or naked, became rampant. Media reports around the time indicate that this was due to a growing public perception of the lack of military capacity to bring about real security to the people. In fact, a scrutiny of media and other NGO reports between 2010 and 2012 suggests widespread fear that the military had not been a neutral arbiter in the conflict (ThisDay, 2010). Many contain allegations of human rights abuses including sexual and gender-based violence. Other reports on perennial crises in Jos allege that, in certain instances, security personnel are linked to powerful vested interests and, therefore, implicated in the prolongation of hostilities (Human Rights Watch, 2001; 2005; 2009). Appendix A contains excerpts of some media reporting during the period January 2010 to December 2012. Two factors lend a certain amount of credence to such assertions. First, in January this year President Goodluck Jonathan had hinted at the infiltration of Boko Haram into critical government institutions. Second, media and anecdotal accounts abound of security personnel posted to Jos owning swelled bank accounts, cars and houses as remuneration for either carrying out direct night attacks in villages or facilitating such attacks by Fulani herdsmen. Furthermore, there is the allegation that in some instances STF commanders provided tacit cover for insurgency attacks by turning a blind eye to intelligence and neglecting to put in place procedural security measures.

Current Situation Analysis

The current situation in Jos and environs is relatively calm and there has been a significant reduction in armed violence. Other characteristics of the present situation are:

- Cessation of bomb blasts mainly due to tight security measures by the STF
- Prevalence of large numbers of arms and offensive weapons in the hands of civilians and organized groups in the communities
- The reluctance among citizens to disarm because of uncertainty of the security situation
- Post-conflict criminality manifested as armed robbery, kidnappings, cattle rustling, use of illicit drugs, etc.
- Cattle rustling has especially led to the escalation of conflict, and is responsible for the manifestation of a similar pattern of violence in the Southern Zone of Plateau State, with pockets of the situation in the Northern and Central Zones
- Continuation of dialogue and peace building activities by different groups, including the STF

- After a brief interlude, the major flash points of Riyom and Barkin Ladi continue to witness night attacks and the attendant killing of villagers in such raids
- Be that as it may, the city is still significantly polarized along religious and ethnic lines in most of the low and average income neighbourhoods. Although trust is gradually returning, this settlement pattern is yet to change.

Literature Review: Conceptualising Security Sector Reform and Conflict Management in the Context of an Emerging Democracy

Security is a key objective pursued by states, human entities and individuals. It means the state of being free from danger or fear; and it enables individual's human rights to be enforced within an environment that enables citizens to thrive with open access to education, human and economic development Bastick et al (2013). Security is closely related to the state, and the state may enhance or impinge its realization. Weaver in (Guzzini et al, 2004, p70) draws attention to the fact drawn from early to modern thinkers, the role of the state in providing security has not changed and security is the chief purpose of government. Weber (1994, p78) sees the state as the sole purveyor of authority that successfully claims the right of legitimate use of physical force within a given territory while the International Commission on intervention and state sovereignty in its report of (2001) believes that responsibility to protect lies first and foremost with the state whose people are directly affected by conflict (ICISS, 2001, para 2). Tadjbakhsh et al (2007) see the state and its agents as responsible and accountable for their acts of commission and omission towards social and economic policies, which can help in reducing poverty, mitigating fear of cruelty and violation of human rights violations. The literature on security sector reform (SSR), a concept that emerged in the late 1990s, portrays an evolution from a largely pre-Cold War statist framework to an agenda more centred on guaranteeing the security of individuals, communities and entire societies. SSR, in this study, refers to,

> The transformation of a nation's security system, which includes all of its actors, their roles, responsibilities and actions, so that it is managed and operated in a manner that is more consistent with democratic norms and sound principles of good governance. (Wulf, 2004:)

This is particularly important for countries, like Nigeria that are transiting from military rule to democratic systems. According to Sedra (2010:16) "security sector reform is a precondition for stability and sustainable development in countries recovering from conflict or making transitions from authoritarianism, fragility or collapse." This is because under authoritarian regimes security agencies operate to protect national interests, narrowly interpreted to imply regime security. Conversely, the overriding goal of SSR is to promote human security. With regard to Nigeria, Fayemi and Olonisakin (2008) argue that,

> The scale, scope, virulence and intensity of conflict in the first eight years of civilian rule demonstrated that there is no teleological link between military disengagement from politics and the deepening of the security sector reform agenda, especially in a state where the values, ethos and principles of governance are still essentially authoritarian.

In fact, Gwamma (2010:6) goes as far as to assert that,

> *The recent radicalisation of religion through violent killings and ethnic crisis using sophisticated weapons, points to the negative hangover of the military on the Nigerian polity.*

After 13 years of democratic experiment, incidents of violent conflict persist in various parts of Nigeria, the most recent and arguably the most serious being the Boko Haram insurgency that has spread from the North East to other regions. Moreover, Nigeria is still in the process of formulating an appropriate National Security Policy to replace the National Defence Policy of the military era. The prevalence and persistence of violent conflict underscore the basic premise of security sector reform which, as Wulf's definition depicts, is concerned with democratising the governance structure as well as building the operational capability of security agencies (Sedra, 2010). Awanen (2013:5) captures the imperative for SSR in Nigeria quite aptly,

> *The continuing inability of the security sector to effectively tackle spiralling violence and acts of terrorism in parts of Nigeria suggests the presence of huge capacity gaps both in the governance and in the operations of the security sector. For instance, there have long been accusations of ineptitude, impunity, extra-judicial killings and corruption against members of the security services. These accusations suggest lack of professionalism among security personnel which could undermine public trust in the security sector. These gaps point to the need for reform of the security sector to improve the governance, efficiency and effectiveness of Nigeria's security agencies.*

The statement indicates that SSR is both a capacity as well as a governance issue. As with pre-Cold War security assistance framework, the need to train and equip all security personnel with appropriate skills and operational tools to bridge the capacity gap is an important aspect of SSR. However, the key concern is to institutionalise a broad-based oversight system rooted in democratic principles for effectively managing, monitoring and holding security sector actors and agencies accountable. Therefore, going by the UN Secretary-General's Report on Security Sector Reform (2008), SSR entails a holistic conceptualisation of what the security sector constitutes beyond the core security agencies to include their legal frameworks, judicial bodies, correctional institutions and government oversight bodies. The Security sector in Nigeria comprises all the institutions and other aspects of the State involved in providing the security of the state and its citizens; these institutions include the State Armed forces, which comprise Armed and Defense Forces, Police, Para-military forces, Intelligence and security services. The State oversight and management bodies which include the executive branch, National Advisory bodies, Parliament, Ministries of Defense, Internal Affairs, Foreign Affairs etc., and the Justice and rule of law institutions. In order for these institutions to adequately serve the population, they must meet the appropriate standards of civilian control, accountability, transparency and rule of law requirements. Security sector reform is meant to be a process that ensures that the institutions of the security are structures that people run to and not run from.

According to Hutton (2010), a comprehensive conceptualisation of SSR means that its primary aim is to "precipitate a broader change relationship between security sector agencies and citizens." Yet, in the Nigerian context, Fayemi and Olonisakin, demonstrate a clear lack of civil society voice in being able to inform security sector reform compounded by an obvious lack of political support for the process. As a result, Nigeria is yet to typify the linkage between security and development. This is particularly the case with regard to the police function in democratising country. Pwajok (2013) sees the police as the organized civil force of the state saddled with the maintenance of law and order, the detection and prevention of crime as part of the duties in internal security, a role supported by the 1999 Constitution. He describes the typical emotions Nigerians have towards the police as feelings of doom, the looming threat of harassment and the guarantee that an individual's rights will probably be violated, sensibilities insulted, and time wasted. He quotes the words of the present Inspector General of Police in his maiden address as he articulates the ills of the Nigerian police to buttress his points:

> The Nigerian police have become commercialized and it provides services at the whims of the highest bidder, with police stations becoming business centres and collection points for rendering returns; the special anti-robbery squads becoming killer teams engaging in deals for land speculators and debt collectors. Illegalities thrive under your watchful eyes because you have compromised the very soul of our profession; our respect is gone and the Nigerian public has lost even the slightest confidence in the ability of the police to do any good thing.

Security sector reform refers to the activities and structures put in place, to improve a country's capability to deliver justice and security in a transparent, accountable and professional manner. When these activities are carried out in a professional manner, these activities may enhance the states capacities to prevent large scale violence committed by non-state perpetrators and mitigate the level in which the state actors become complicit in perpetrating such atrocities (PeaceBrief, 144, 2013).

Sedra (2010) cautions that the scope and goals of SSR maybe too ambitious, and therefore inappropriate, for the complex and intractable conflicts that exist in many parts of the world with specific reference to Asia, the Middle East and Sub-Saharan Africa. This is not to suggest that SSR should be abandoned in its entirety. But, Sedra argues that a more nuanced approach that takes adequate cognizance of the multi-layered politico-strategic dimensions of conflict is required. This is because security intervention and SSR take place in the context of intricate, and often incompatible, political, economic and socio-cultural interests. To some extent, Sedra's argument is motivated by an observation that SSR is predominantly driven by western liberal democratic theory and practice, without due regard to important complexities in local contexts. In his opinion textbook SSR is more suitable to societies with fairly strong democratic institutions than to fragile states with deep-rooted conflicts.

For instance, in the Nigerian setting, violent conflicts are triggered, fuelled and sustained by a multiplicity of interacting factors such as struggle over economic and/or political resources, identity-based grievances and ideological incongruities. Such factors tend to be intricately interwoven, deep-rooted and to produce intractable conflicts, particularly where issues had been repressed under authoritarian rule (Gwamma, 2010). In these situations, conflict transformation responses require sufficient local knowledge and expertise. Hence, Ball (2010) argues that genuine SSR must be anchored on local demand and be driven by local stakeholders rather than pandering to a donor-funded agenda. This entails a proper assessment of how security agencies have responded in time of conflict from the perspectives of those nearest to it. It also calls for a determination of how violent conflict and the actions of security agencies to manage it have impacted on their lives.

Given the non-applicability of conventional SSR to every context, an important issue for this study is to explore the possibility of developing a context-specific SSR toolkit suitable to the Nigerian context. Fayemi and Olonisakin make an initial effort in this direction by suggesting six elements that must form part of any discussion on improving security sector governance in Nigeria. These involve a proper understanding of the political context (national framework), as noted earlier. In this regard, Akinwale (2008) argues that the Nigerian political system depicts a coexistence of modern and traditional values. Thus, he concludes that an integration of modern and traditional conflict management strategies need to be institutionalised as part of a general SSR strategy. According to Fayemi and Olonisakin a review of the laws, policies and regulations governing the conduct of security agencies (legal framework), and the system of controlling their financial resources (financial management) are also vital.

Sedra insists that public sector finance management (PFM) standards and practices need to be built into SSR in a manner that is transparent to ensure fiscal sustainability as well as accountability. Other elements concern an examination of the roles of non-state actors in conflict situations, the professional stance of security agencies in terms of training and operational capability, and the level of legislative, bureaucratic and civil society oversight (accountability). These elements coincide with SSR components highlighted by Sedra and Ball in order to make them more amenable to diverse settings. In addition, Ebo (2010) stresses the importance of bridging the gap between citizens and security sector agencies in line with United Nations good SSR practices, which emphasise grassroots participation and ownership. Ebo also underlines the need for all aspects and stakeholders in the sector to work in synergy to achieve a successful SSR process. Over the years, a significant amount of literature has developed on the Jos conflict. Many of the researchers have been attracted by the protracted nature of the conflict, the scale of violence and the sluggishness of intervention strategies in response to it. The researchers also come from a variety of sources such as academics, civil society and non-governmental organizations, faith-based groups, security agencies, and even governmental actors, among others. To the extent that the researchers are from different sources, they also each try to highlight different priorities. Be that as it may, many have been interested in the causes of the conflict, the parties and dynamics of the conflict, intervention strategies, among others. The earliest works covering the period from 2001 to 2008 are sketchy, and they try to investigate the causes of the conflict, the different actors, their positions, interests and needs in the conflict, as well as the perceptions of the parties.

Another common factor in these works is the historical evolution and chronology of the conflict. Among such works are Human Rights Watch Reports (2001, 2006, 2009), Danfulani and Fwatshak (2002), Adetula (2005), Omotola (2006), Best (2007), and Gwamna (2010). The scope and analyses of these works and others in their category was informed by the need to provide basic information about the conflict and a lead for interveners seeking solutions to the conflict. Danfulani and Fwatshak (2005), Goshit (2006), Best (2007), and PIDAN (2010) have particularly been interested in the history of the conflict. This is because the conflict parties base their perspectives from a number of historical issues. These historical analyses, even though often controversial, have helped to build a significant background to the conflict. Unlike the other researchers done by scholars, PIDAN is a confederation of community-based organizations in Plateau State and brings out the community perspective to the conflict. Yoroms (2000) brings a regional, middle belt perspective to the conflict and places it within the contexts of similar conflicts in the middle belt region. Egwu (2009) comes in with a similar middle belt angle in trying to analyse the issues in the conflict and define a way forward. Kwaja (2011), Kruse (2011) and Africa Report No. 196(2012) look at institutional factors and the inability to address these issues as a causal link.

Some of the researchers have been interested in the role of the state and its types of intervention in the conflict. Omotola (2006) picks on the use of the State of Emergency to end the crisis, and concludes that the policy did not focus on the causes of the conflict, and so it failed. A number of NGOs have come into Jos with a view to intervening in the crisis. Their sought interventions have led to the emergence and production of some important research reports and publications. The Friedrich Ebert Stiftung research by Higazi looks at the conflict in Jos as politically inspired and xenophobic. The CORDAID research by Ostein (2009) is perhaps one of the most insightful outsider perspectives, as well as a controversial report. It reduces the conflict to the Governor Jang and the Jasawa as an ethnic community and then puts most of the analyses within this paradigm. Others are Best and Hoomlong (2011) looking at the role of faith-based organizations in post conflict transformation; while Para-Mallam (2011) focuses on the search for durable peace in Plateau state.

Finally, the literature underscores the human rights dimension to SSR. For instance, in virtually all cases of security forces intervention in peace keeping worldwide, incidents of sexual and gender-based violence are rampant and severe. In Nigeria, the prevalence of SGBV as well as other forms of abuse and brutality by security personnel, particularly the police, has long been a basis of calls for reform by civil society groups such as NOPRIN (Network on Policy Reform in Nigeria).

Methodology

The study relied on a combined qualitative and quantitative strategy to centralize in-depth participatory research and learning in addition to broad survey investigation. This approach was considered most suitable for promoting a comprehensive understanding of the precise content of the roles of key actors and the complex contexts in which they act and which they create and re-create. Qualitative methods involved the documentary analysis of media, official government and other organizational reports to shed light on government decisions and security sector operations in relation to the Jos conflict. Twenty-five key informant interviews were held with critical security sector actors in and outside the STF. Key informants also included opinion moulders from other segments of society such as traditional, religious, community, women and youth leaders, and political actors.

To assess community level experiences and perspectives, five Focus Group Discussions (FGDs) were conducted with various indigenous and settler groups spread across the five LGAs. For a deeper understanding of the effects of military intervention in the Jos conflict, the study explored the life histories five (5) individuals (two Muslims and three Christians) in their communities (one per LGA) who are victims/survivors of violent crises. This method helped to map the context and trajectory of personal experiences. The quantitative survey method involved 485 (of the proposed 500) structured interviews with residents in urban, semi-urban and rural areas in the five LGAs under study. Table 1 displays the distribution of respondents by LGA. The structured interviews sought to investigate the perspectives and experiences of various ethno-religious constituencies during and after episodes of violence.

Table 1: Distribution of Respondents by Local Government Area

Residential LGA	Frequency	Percentage
Barkin Ladi	57	11.8
Jos East	38	7.8
Jos North	187	38.6
Jos South	147	30.3
Riyom	56	11.5
Total	485	100

Discussion and Analysis of Findings

Operational rules of engagement and responses of the Special Task Force in the context of the Jos conflict The precise operational rules of engagement of military formations are normally classified and not released for public consumption. However, from documentary analysis of unpublished reports, studies and from interviews and interactive sessions with top-level security personnel it was possible to deduce some of the ground rules that informed Jos operations. The military troops deployed to Plateau State in the immediate aftermath of violent outbreak consisted of soldiers. However, possibly due to public outcry over ethno-religious polarisation within the military, the Federal Government soon set up a Special Joint Military Task Force. The STF is composed of the Nigerian Army, Navy, Airforce, Police, Nigerian Security and Civil Defence Corps (NSCDC) and Department of State Security Services. The police component consists of the mobile police and the Special Investigation Bureau (SIB). All members of the STF wear the same uniform with badges for identification. It is important to note that reports of 'fake soldiers' attacking civilians caused the federal government had to order an entire modification of STF uniforms.

A top-level police officer at the Command Headquarters reported a high level of collaboration between the police and the STF and among its constituent parts, however not without occasional altercations. For example, in March 2013 a Muslim soldier who was part of an STF contingent stationed in Michang in Plateau South was reported to have shot and killed a Christian policeman on the team. The matter threatened to degenerate into a shootout between the soldiers and the police and fuel tensions in the surrounding area if not for the quick intervention of the STF Commander and the Commissioner of Police. Nevertheless, the police officer interviewed maintained that there was a high level of synergy in the operations. With regard to how long before the police take over responsibility for the internal security of Jos and environs from the STF he replied,

> *It was supposed to be a forty-five-day affair but look at! It has gone to three and a half years now. Nobody can really foretell, I believe that the complementary [military] action at the Federal Government level over the Boko Haram issue and other things is prolonging the matter. I think we are getting to the end of the crisis. (Senior Police Officer/ Interview, 28/02/2013).*

In addition to the STF, amidst allegations of a Jihadist agenda by the STF under the leadership of the first General Officer Commanding (GOC) the 3rd Armoured Division in Jos, Major General Sale Maina, the Plateau State Government made moves to set up Operation Rainbow. This is a security outfit headed by a retired military officer of Plateau origin established to guarantee security to villages in Barkin Ladi and Riyom LGAs. These villages had witnessed substantial raids of homes and farmlands by Fulani herdsmen and 'faceless' gunmen who were rumoured to be either STF personnel or 'fake soldiers'. Operation Rainbow was mandated to collaborate with the STF to restore peace and maintain law and order. The general mandate given to the STF was,

> *To restore law and order in aid to civil authority and to protect law abiding citizens and commuters on federal and major roads in Plateau and parts of Bauchi States.*

In the opinion of security personnel interviewed this mandate has largely been fulfilled. As a top-level officer of the STF pointed out, citing a speech made by Prof Ignatius Elaigwu, "You cannot not restore peace; you can only restore law and order," which the STF mandate stipulates. With the return of normal commercial activities and movement of goods and persons around Jos metropolis, and to some extent the surrounding areas, he and other security personnel interviewed believed the job had essentially been accomplished. Still, they were of the opinion that the police still lacked the competence to deal with recurrent threats of terrorist activity that persisted in some parts of the state. In the words of the senior police interviewee,

> *The situation has gone beyond normal accepted practice. When people are coming with sophisticated weapons, guns, and ground-to-air missiles and all kinds of things. We have to seek support from the military to do the military operation while we take care of the civil operation [...] Like I was called some two days ago that somewhere in the Angwa Rogo area, hey recovered a large cache of explosion, ready to be exploded; large quantity, with remote control, batteries, everything. (Senior Police Officer/ Interview, 28/02/2013)*

The key rules of engagement could be summarised as follows:

1. Maintain the principle of minimum force and proportionality at all times.
2. Use of force should be a last resort after every reasonable effort to contain a situation had been made.

3. Use of force should only be resorted to if other means had failed or if non-use of force would result in the death or grievous injury to security personnel. For example, where there is evidence of a hostile act or hostile act.1

4. Use of force must be limited in intensity and duration and must be employed as a protective measure.

5. Decision to open fire must only be upon the order of the on-scene commander unless there is no sufficient time to obtain such an order.

6. Fire must be controlled and aimed at non-vital body parts in order not to kill.

7. Avoid collateral damage.

8. Render medical assistance and record deaths at incident after cessation of fire. Data gathered to be passed through appropriate chain of command.

9. Protect internally displaced persons (IDPs) and assist agencies engaged in the distribution of relief materials.

10. Undertake activities that would aid in diffusing tension.

11. The above-stated rules of engagement are standard parameters that conform to international guidelines on the conduct of military operations to contain civil strife.

However, they do not contain specific instructions regarding civil-military interactions to guide the behaviour of STF members stationed among the various communities. For instance, there is no reference to issues of human rights and sexual conduct. Furthermore, assertions of military complicity in perpetrating ethno-religious violence raise a number of questions: What efforts were made to ensure these rules were made known to all security personnel, and to the general public? What grievance and complaints channels were made available to the public to report infractions? What sanctions were put in place and imposed against defaulters?

According to a top-level military officer interviewed during the field research, a knowledge gap with regard to standard operational procedures (SOP) was observed and began to be addressed mid-2012 through in mission training. He explained that the gap existed due to the different training backgrounds of the various services making up the STF, some of who were not averse to indiscriminate use of firearms. He cited the following example, Some of the police shoot to the air. The day they were going, right here in our headquarters, they were shooting to the air and I asked: 'what happened?'

> They said because the police are happy so they shoot bullets to the air. You do not do that as a soldier because you will have to account for the bullet rounds. In the Police, because they do not account for the rounds, they can afford to shoot into the air and enjoy themselves. (Senior Military Officer/Interview, 22/02/2013)

1Hostile act refers to an action where the intent is to cause death, bodily harm or destruction of designated properties. Hostile intent refers to threat of imminent use of force, which is demonstrated through an action, which appears to be preparatory to a hostile act.

The STF has consistently refuted claims of military misconduct and complicity in ethno-religious violence, at least officially. However, in the interview with the senior military officer above, it became clear that the STF has received numerous petitions from the public containing allegations of misconduct and maltreatment by STF personnel. Since 2012, panels of investigation were set up to process petitions in certain cases leading to disciplinary action, including dismissal. However, he admitted that the media does not usually report this and so the public is largely unaware of measures taken to address violations.

Roles played by the Special Task Force and its constituent agencies in the Jos conflict

This section examines the roles played by the STF from the perspectives and experiences of residents in the five LGAs under study since 2010. It weaves media reports on the roles played by various security agencies, notably the STF, with the perspectives of research participants in structured and semi structured interviews and FGDs. It also considers changes in respondents' attitudes towards military intervention since January 2010 till date based on their perspectives or experiences in relation to the conduct of the STF. In addition, it discusses the views of various key informants on the conduct of security agencies and their suggestions on SSR. In looking at the role of the security agencies and their intervention on the Jos Plateau, records show that the military have actually been in the state since September 2001. On Monday 12 September 2011, President Jonathan gave an order for the STF under the Chief of Defence Staff to take full charge of security operations in Plateau State.

Allegations of Complicity by Security Forces: The Joint Task Force With that announcement, all the security outfits namely the Air Force, Army, SSS and the police would now be under the military authorities. Prior to that order, the Military had been in Jos since 2008, under the command of the General Officer Commanding the 3rd Division; General Saleh Maina who had also excused the police from certain duties and said only the military would be in charge. The opposition to military presence in Plateau state grew fierce as the GOC was accused of taking sides in the conflict and identity cards of some officers were found on some scenes of violence, the Federal Government then designated the Special Task Force to handle security matters of the state and separating it from the office of the GOC. In the process, the state Governor applied to the President to seek approval to set up the state security outfit called Operation Rainbow with a retired Air vice Marshal to head it, in a bid to complement the role of the police and the STF (Weekly Trust, 2011, p.6). Accusations and counter accusations of alleged partisanship, non-neutrality and direct involvement by security personnel on either side of the conflict divide have characterized the Jos crisis. Even though this has been the case, and although the case has been repeatedly highlighted and touches on the heart of the Nigerian state and its federalism, very little research has been carried out on this problem. This is partly due to the fact that security forces are typically defensive of their personnel and choose internal, non-transparent and non-publicly accountable methods to deal with such episodes when they occur. Furthermore, researchers are not granted access to details of episodes involving unprofessional conduct by security personnel.

The outbreaks of crisis in the city of Jos from 2001 till date seem to have a re-occurring trend with the security arrangement. Once an outbreak of hostilities commences, there always seems to be a notable absence of security personnel, while the few military personnel available either have no clear operational orders on the rule of engagement or sometimes take part in killings on both sides of the divide. The Sunday Standard (p.8, 2010) carried such an item its reportage of the Bukuru crisis, pointing to the inability of the military to intervene, with perpetrators killing and looting and burning properties in the full glare of the security agents. This indifference angers peace loving citizens who anticipate prompt intervention by the security forces.

The Weekly Trust of September 2011 in their cover story also carried indictments against both police and the military; the writers of the story portray how the security agencies are viewed by both sides of the divide. The police are accused of being used by the Christian dominated state government and so if seen around the Muslim dominated areas, the police are likely going to be attacked and killed; while the soldiers are being accused of being used by federal government to deploy mainly Muslims to Jos who side with their own in the cause of carrying out their duties. With such sentiments running high, many soldiers have been sacked by the hostility of host communities from areas such as Heipang, Barkin Ladi, Riyom and Kuru. This level of distrust from the citizenry leveled at the security agencies has led many of the citizens to take the law into their hands on the assumption that no institution of government can guarantee them security. In almost all the attacks in the villages of Riyom and Barkin Ladi; ethnic cleansing in Heipang, simultaneous attacks in Kuru, Babale and Foron there have been allegations of the involvement of the soldiers, a situation which has done much damage to image and credibility of the soldiers. The invasion of Mahanga which is the base of the mercenaries; by the STF after series of attacks had been waged against the villages of Barkin Ladi and Riyom and the discovery of large amounts of sophisticated weapons moved into this base, which was beamed on NTA network news under the STF command seems to indict the complicity of the military. In a write up in the Nigerian Standard of December 12, 2008, the reporter Ayuba in an article titled "Police Transfers: a plot against Plateau", the author highlighted the victimization of non-Hausa Muslims in the Nigeria Police Force in other to pave the way for Northern police officers. Others are the suppressions of promotions of police officers simply, because of not being of the region and faith. He traced a precedence of transfer of indigenous police officers out of Jos subsequent to the 2001 crisis, which was re-enacted in the 2008 crisis. The Special Task Force deployed to Jos since 2010 has had changes in its leadership; and ethnic and religious actors have tried to associate the leadership of these task forces with the level of violence or otherwise suffered in the crisis. Often, the suspicion is linked to the faith of the commanders. Major General Saleh Maina headed the first Special Task Force Operation Safe Haven from 2009 till 2010. His tenure was extremely controversial as it witnessed intense sectarian division among the troops as well as the populace. It was also during his tenure that the Dogo na Hawa night massacre of dozens of non-Muslim women and children took place in March 2010. His tenure will also be remembered for prohibiting police personnel and police patrol vehicles from patrolling the streets at certain hours of the day, thereby suspending the Constitutional role of the police in the maintenance of law and order. It was a total military operation. In an earlier advertorial carried in the Sunday Standard of January 31, 2009, the Coalition of Plateau Youth Forum wrote an open to the President, Federal Republic of Nigeria demanding the removal of General Saleh Maina; citing his alleged deliberate involvement and complicity in the crisis in Jos. The general loss of trust and confidence in his handling of the security situation, the choice of officers involved in the operation, the rules of engagement and the deployment of troops deployed within Jos and Bukuru were brought against his leadership. They further alleged having evidence to show against him and demanded he should be brought before a tribunal. Major Saleh Maina in his book, The Image of the Military in Conflict Management has posited that the involvement of the military in internal crises is as a result of perpetrators of violence using superior weapons and tactics beyond police competence to curtail the crisis. This necessitated the involvement of the mobile police and subsequently the military who carry out these secondary role guided by their code of conduct. He debunks the alleged complicity of the military in Jos as being subject to personal and group interpretations which are bound to be subjective; he indicts the media of partisanship and lop-sidedness in geographical location and posits that accusations and attacks on the military do not stem from genuine and tangible reasons. The issues of the Nigerian military being partisan, he believes are mere fabrications because of the eclectic nature of the composition of the soldiers and states that appointments and postings are not made on the basis of primordial parameters but based on competence, merit, proficiency and service exigencies.

The former Chief of Army Staff, Lt General Abdulrahaman Danbazzau, who led the operations in Jos after the November 2008 crisis was also accused by the Berom Youth movement in a press conference at the NUJ. He was alleged to have directed Muslim military men to protect only Hausa areas during the crisis of January 2010, which engulfed Jos North and Jos South LGAs. According to a leader of the BYM interviewed ( ), the organisation believed that such a directive contributed to the brutal killing of Christians by Muslim military men during the mayhem. In the press conference, the spokesman for the BYM also called for the investigation into the use of military uniforms by the Hausa-Fulani's during crisis. (Sunday Standard, p16, 2010). This was, however, during the embryonic years of the deployment of the military to internal security operations in Jos. In the years that followed and with wider deployment and longer stay of security agents in the same locations, the accusations got deeper and more worrisome. The accusations against security personnel began to take firm root with the incessant night attacks on local communities in five local government areas of Plateau North, namely Jos North, Jos South, Riyom, Barkin Ladi and, to a lesser extent, Bassa. A number of key informants speculated that the attacks could have been the work of 'fake soldiers' wearing stolen military uniforms. But, the attacks often portrayed a level of professionalism involving the use of combat military-type offensive weapons and, in some instances, identity cards of military personnel were found at the scenes of attack. In addition, attackers used the same Hilux vans employed by military personnel. Attacks in Farin Lamba, which took place within two weeks from the 25 of January 2011 along the Kaduna Vom road left a death toll of 30 victims, were alleged to have been carried out by men in military uniform driving a patrol van belonging to the Special Task Force. In the aftermath of that attack, women trooped out in hundreds in Vom and called for the removal of the Commander, General Hassan Umar. The State Commissioner of Police, Mr. Abdulrahaman Akano confirmed that some people in military uniform in a Hilux went to Farin Lamba between eight and nine pm on the said day and killed five people. Failure to unearth episodes of this nature served to erode the confidence of local communities in the security personnel and their activities.

The response of the Nigerian Armed Forces is often to change their personnel and deploy new soldiers to replace those who have served for a long periods of time. Even this is grossly inadequate because it occurs too far and in between. The redeployments, for instance followed the protest of thousands of women clad in black, holding placards reading "soldiers have a hidden agenda in

Plateau", "soldiers are hired killers" and asking the federal government to withdraw the soldiers from the state. The Chief of Army staff Brigadier Ihejirika in addressing the newly drafted soldiers in Plateau State in February 2011, admonished them not to take sides in the conflict but to be impartial in the discharge of their duties. With so much outcry and distrust levelled at the security agencies, the federal government has been trying to wade into the matter by making different changes at the highest command levels. The presidential order of taking over the security operatives through the STF was the initial response aimed at bringing this parallel security structures under the military authority. However, the state government sponsored Operation Rainbow, coexist with the STF along with community vigilantes, all in a bid to secure lives and tackle the crisis. Kaze, a member of the House of Representatives from Jos East Constituency challenged Major General Saleh Maina led STF over its complicity in the handling of the Jos crises that led to the death of hundreds. He argued that the leadership under Maina had done incalculable damage to the image of the military in Plateau State. On the other hand, however, he commended the leadership of Ihejirika and General Sunday Idoko for their different styles of handling of the Jos crises. As highlighted, leadership styles affected the escalation and de-escalation of violence. Unlike the General Maina and General Hassan Umar eras, Major General O. Oshinowo's command of the STF from September 2011 to February 2012, saw a respite in the incessant attacks and ethno-religious violence in Plateau State and its environs. He combined his assignment with dialogue and other conciliatory approaches that brought about a significant decline in night attacks against rural communities. He also left the perpetrators in no doubt about his determination to use maximum force against them. Major General Ibrahim was the fifth STF Commander, and His leadership was characterized by high rate of attacks, which was intense and appeared to be targeted at two local government areas of Barkin Ladi and Riyom. His tenure was brief and disastrous for rural communities in Riyom and Barkin Ladi in particular. It also witnessed the resurgence of terrorist bombings in Christian places of worship in Jos, with occasional reprisal attacks. The fact that killings continued unabated in spite of the emergency rule declared on the affected local governments remained a silent indictment. General Henry Ayoola is the sixth commander and presently in charge of the STF. He inherited the era of night rural attacks that appeared to overwhelm his command for some time. The zenith of the crisis under his leadership were the attacks by armed groups stationed in the mountains of Riyom and Barkin Ladi LGAs, the attack on Maseh and other villages in July 2012 which led to the killing of dozens of local people, including Senator Gyang Danton and the Majority Leader in the Plateau State House of Assembly Gyang Fulani. The situation gradually improved towards the end of 2012 through the use of conciliation and dialogue between the warring groups, with the support of Senator Gyang Pwajok.

The review looked at the security sector in its interventionist role in Plateau and its impact and ability to secure and protect lives has been marred by allegations of lack of neutrality, there is need for security reform and internal operations to be ad hoc and brief because when soldiers are deployed for too long, they tend to be dragged into issues of unprofessional conduct. Findings from structured interviews, as shown in Fig. 2 indicate that immediately the military were deployed to Jos 83.1% of participants were initially either very happy (63.1%) or relieved (20%). Only 16.9% were either indifferent (3.1%), sad (6.6%) or had mixed feelings (7.2%). At that time, respondents' expectations that the STF would restore peace and security to the area were for the most part either very high (40.8%) or high (28%). Only 21.3% had low (9.8%) or very low (11.5%) expectations of military intervention. On the other hand, the data shows a significant change as portrayed in Fig. 3 where 46.7% of respondents currently have either a negative (16.7%) or very negative (30.1%) attitude towards military presence.

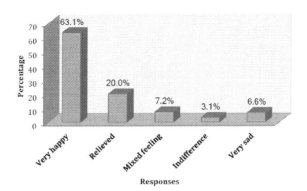

Fig. 2: Feelings of respondents when the Federal Government first sent in the military to intervene as a result of the ethno-religious violence that broke out in Jos in January 2010

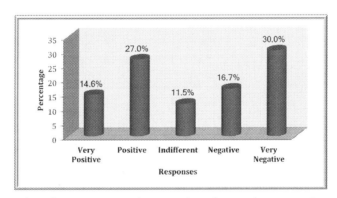

Fig. 3: Respondents' current attitude towards military presence in Jos and environs

Against the backdrop of the evolution of events after military deployment, findings from the structured interviews suggest a number of possible explanations for the change. First, 57.2% of respondents felt that the presence of the STF in Jos had actually either increased insecurity (26.6%), made no difference at all (11.8%) or only brought about security temporarily (18.8%), postponing violence till a later time. The figure was slightly higher at 58.5% with regard to the level of security in respondents' own locality where respondents said the presence of the STF had either increased insecurity (26.4%), made no difference at all (17.9%) or only brought about security temporarily (14.2%). Virtually all key informants reiterated the view that the security agencies had merely brought temporary respite as underlying issues at the root of ethno-religious conflict were yet to be resolved. In the words of a Muslim women leader, "The security forces are only suppressing the issues, but the issues are still there and are becoming more complicated" (Interview, 25/03/2013).

A Second possible explanation relates to the connection between respondents' perspectives on the level of effectiveness of the STF in relation to certain indicators. For instance, Fig. 4 reveals that 48.4% of respondents assessed the STF to have been minimally effective (20.6%) or not effective at all (27.8%) compared to a fairly similar proportion (44.8%) who judged it to have been quite effective (28.7%) or highly effective, while 6.8% were unsure.

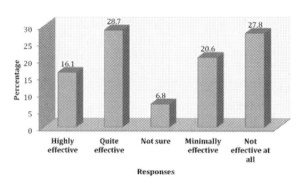

Fig. 4: Respondents' assessment of level of effectiveness of the STF

Key informants generally associated the effectiveness, or lack of it, to factors inherent and extraneous to the STF. Inherent factors include the presence of bad eggs among security agents in terms of corruption or ethnoreligious prejudice. For example, with regard to the latter, the President of the Jasawa Development Association (JDA) complained about bias in the composition of the Plateau State Security Council,

> *There is no single Muslim in the state security meeting. Ranging from the governor of the state, the GOC, commissioner of police, director of SSS, STF Commander, Operation Rainbow Commandant etc., are all Christians. With these kinds of arrangement, why won't we be prone to the danger of insecurity? Do you think our people are secured? No, because whenever decisions on security issues are taken it would favour them since no body to protect our own interest (Interview, 29/03/2013).*

The President of the Pentecostal Fellowship of Nigeria (PFN), had a similar complaint,

> *We have had different [military] leaders...There were those that were not friendly, they came as agents to support the Muslims. There were those who were fair and neutral in the crises, supporting neither the Muslims, Christians or pagans in order to ensure peace […] Not much has been done in the area [of justice] because there has been no prosecution of those arrested. For instance, six years ago Muslim youths were arrested, taken Abuja and released...Unfortunately, the same does not apply to our youths who were arrested, some in their homes, and dragged away by security agencies.*

Besides prejudice, Fig.5 indicates that survey respondents also identified internal factors such as taking bribes (30.3%), taking sides based on religion (29.1%) and ethnicity (23.1%), lack of professional competence (14.2%), lack of inter-agency synergy (10.1%) and intelligence gap (6.2%). As the figure also shows, extraneous factors identified by respondents for lack of STF effectiveness in providing security, centred primarily on wider issues in the socio-political context such as the constitutional indigene/settler divide, and the failure of governance (more detail on this below). Other socio-political context factors revolved around the words and actions of political actors within and outside Plateau State and those of traditional and religious leaders.

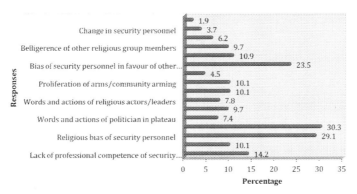

Fig. 5: Respondents' current attitude towards military presence in Jos and environs

Respondents' change in attitude towards security agencies is also a result of negative behaviour observed in the conduct of security personnel in terms of their treatment of the citizenry. Aside from taking bribes, many respondents mentioned acts like brutality, sexual violence and other human rights violations. It is important here to note the variations in findings according to LGA with regard to the forms of misconduct enumerated. This will be discussed under the next section on the effects of STF presence in the various LGAs. However, it is also important to highlight certain positive roles that respondents ascribed to the STF. FGDs held in the three LGAs of Barkin Ladi, Jos North and Riyom revealed that the STF, under General Ayoola's tenure launched another aspect of Operation Safe Haven through the community service activities. These include advocacy strategies to encourage the people to lay down their arms, free medical facilities and services, provision of improved seedlings, organizing seminars and parleys for youth in the crisis-ridden communities. The STF recently rehabilitated 25 boreholes in various crisis-ridden communities in. These have helped to build the confidence and trust of the host communities in the force. The interview with the top-level STF officer confirmed that the STF had stepped up such activities since 2012. He cited specific examples of facilitating dialogue/negotiations between belligerent or hostile parties, youth training and empowerment schemes, community sensitisation and community assistance. However, some interviewees were of the opinion that such STF interventions had been one-sided. Fig. 6 reveals that 28.7% of respondents credited the STF for rescuing people for danger, 26.4% for stopping the killings, 23.5% for making people feel safer and 21% for carrying out peace building activities.

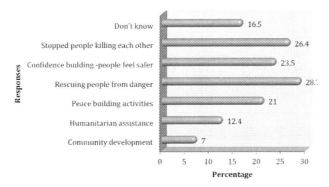

Fig. 6: Positive Roles Played by the STF

Effects of the presence of the Special Task Force on residents of the five LGAs under study All research participants reported multifaceted and traumatic effects of violent conflict on themselves or on people they knew. Among survey respondents, Fig. 7 reveals that 71.3% had lost someone to violence. They lost children (5.6%), parents (6.4%), sibling (16.1%), other relatives (16.3%), friends (26.6%), neighbours (21.9%), business partners (6.2%), and colleagues (9.7%).

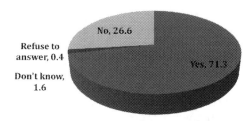

Fig. 7: Have you lost anybody to violent conflict in Jos since 2010?

In addition, as depicted in Fig. 8, 62.7% of respondents reported the loss of property, livelihoods, friendships (due to disrupted social relationships), educational opportunities and bodily integrity (owing to sexual abuse).

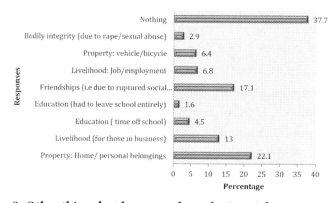

Fig. 8: Other things lost by respondents during violent crises in Jos

participants and respondents breaking down in tears as the recounted their experiences. In Riyom LGA one discussant said,

> After a man host a soldier in his own house, gave him place to sleep so as to protect him and his property, it is that same soldier that ended up killing the man that hosted him. This is a practical situation that happened here and in most neighbouring communities. Usually when they kill anyone they are immediately transferred out of another location overnight so that before you report the culprit they are nowhere to be found. (FGD, 28/07/2013).

In Jos North LGA (FGD, 29/07/2013), One of the respondents gave an incident where he was attacked by the military until the youths in the area intervened before he was allowed to go. Some of the most severe negative effects listed by youth who participated in the discussion include:

i. Exposed to taking hard drugs to build resistance to fear
ii. Proliferations of arms for self-defence
iii. Unemployment
iv. Rising youth violence and lawlessness because they resorted to taking laws into their hands since they do not trust the government for protection
v. Homelessness
vi. Excessive rise in the cost of accommodation and shops.

In Jos South LGA (FGD, 25/07/2013), a discussant declared, "We have lost our friends, business partners, family, neighbours and colleagues." Another respondent claimed the Jos crisis had affected his trust for people because people he called his friends turned out to be the perpetrators of the crisis. Yet another claimed he had been hit personally by the Jos crises in the aspect of business. One discussant even had not been able to recover financially since his shop was burnt down and lives in constantly fear of the re-emergence of violence. Major effects of violent conflict mentioned during FGDs in Barkin Ladi LGA (26/07/2013) involved economic decline since people could no longer go to the farm or move about freely. Sustained night raids had also reduced village populations substantially and instilled fear in those remaining. Religious and ethnic intolerance had also increased. Similar issues were echoed in Jos East LGA (FGD, 27/07/2013), where people claimed to have been financially crippled due to inability to farm. Women, in particular, spoke about the financial strain of having to cope without husbands, sons and other breadwinners who had been killed during crises.

Summary of Key Findings

Findings from the study suggest the following:

- Peoples' views and experiences of the role of security agencies vary widely according to leadership of the STF and residential area.
- Some Commanders, and other security personnel are viewed to have been professional and patriotic. Others exhibited ethno-religious prejudice in the discharge of official functions, causing a severe credibility deficit.
- In recent times, some sector commanders and other security agents found to be complicit in the conflict have been removed and disciplined.
- In some instances, religion was found to be a factor in people's evaluation of the performance of security agents as respondents displayed a high degree of sensitivity to the religious affiliation of the STF Commander and the religious composition of STF platoons.
- In all five LGAs studied there were several allegations of ethnoreligious one-sidedness in the conduct of some security personnel through collusion with vested interest groups to perpetuate violence and insecurity.
- Negative effects of the Jos conflict and prolonged military stay include: sexual exploitation and violence; feelings of victimisation and injustice; residential polarization of Christians

and Muslims; increased youth alcoholism and drug use; traumatisation, depopulation and displacement of rural communities.

- Deep animosities remain between the Fulani nomadic communities and the indigenous Berom. The Fulani accuse the Berom of rustling their cattle. The latter accuse the Fulani of collaborating with Hausa Muslims to carry out a Jihadist agenda as well as a policy of dispossession and occupation to extend grazing lands.
- Although residents in urban centres feel relatively safe, in the rural areas farmers still live in fear of attack at night and when they go to farm. Several people have been displaced and many farmlands have been destroyed.
- Recourse to alternative militaristic and 'spiritual' measures for guaranteeing personal safety by some citizens underscores the urgent need for security sector reform.
- Confidence-building strategies by the STF, civil society and faith-based organisations and community self-efforts have helped to restore peaceful coexistence in certain locations.
- The lack of broad-based civil society oversight mechanisms in the security sector architecture gives the federal and military authorities stronger leverage than the State civilian authority.
- The current security sector framework entrenches the militarisation of public order and undermines the role civil policing, as well as the legitimacy of the entire security apparatus.

Policy Implications for Security Sector Reform

Key policy implications for security sector reform that emerged from the research findings indicate that:

- Nigeria needs to expedite action on a comprehensive National Security Policy. The process for its formulation and approval should be widely consultative.
- Urgent and effective security sector reform is required to build the operational capacity of security agencies in the following areas:
- Capacity building towards strengthening civil and community policing. This would also serve to strengthen democratic governance in the maintenance of internal security
- Strengthening of the Mobile Police Unit to serve as an intermediate force for the speedy restoration of law and order in the event of large-scale violence
- Re-inculcation of professional ethics and inclusion of human rights education and psychological profiling in the training curricular of security personnel
- The institutionalisation of practical mechanisms for interagency collaboration at the level of joint training and intelligence sharing
- Security Sector Reform must incorporate accessible and secure grievance channels to process citizens' reports of violations in the conduct of security operations and personnel.
- Civilian oversight of military operations must include a statutory role for civil society voice and participation to minimise skewed political interference.
- A comprehensive and equitable compensation strategy is required to ensure effective conflict transformation in Plateau State.

Bibliography

Akinwale, A. A. (2008) "Integrating the traditional and the modern conflict management strategies in Nigeria".

Akinwumi, O., Okpeh O, and Gwamna J.D (eds). Inter-Group Relations in Nigeria during the 19th and 20th Centuries. Makurdi, Ibadan. Aboki Publisher. 471-489

Alubo, O (2008) Ethnic Conflict and Citizenship Crisis in the Central region, Ibadan, Programme on Ethnic and Federal studies (PEFS)

Ambe-Uva, T (2010) "Identity Politics and the Jos Crisis: Evidence, Lessons and Challenges of good Governance" in African Journal of History and Culture (AJHC) Vol. 2(3), pp. 42-52, April 2010

Awanem, A. (2013) "Nigeria's Security Sector Reform and the Transformation Agenda." Unpublished Long Essay for Senior Executive Course of the National Institute for Policy and Strategic Studies. Kuru.

Ball, N (2010) "The Evolution of the Security Sector Reform Agenda" in Mark Sedra (ed.) The Future of Security Sector Reform. The Centre for International Governance Innovation (CIGI), Waterloo, Ontario, Canada (www.cigionline.org)

Best, S.G. (2001) "Religion and Religious Conflicts in Northern Nigeria". University of Jos Journal of Political Science. 2 (3). December 2001. 63 – 81.

Best, S.G (2007) Conflict and Peace Building in Plateau State, Nigeria Ibadan, Spectrum books limited

Best, S and Hoomlong, K (2011). Faith Based Organisations and Conflict Transformation in Nigeria. John Archers Publishers.

Best, S and Hoomlong, K (2011) Blench, R and Dendo, M (2003) Acess Rights and conflict over common pool resources on the Jos Plateau, Report to World Bank/ UNDP/DFID-JEWEL (Jigawa Enhancement of Wetlands Livelihood Project).

Bryd, W. A (2010) "The Financial Dimension of Security Sector Reform" in Mark Sedra (ed.) The Future of Security Sector Reform. The Centre for International Governance Innovation (CIGI), Waterloo, Ontario, Canada (www.cigionline.org)

Ebo, A and Powell, K (2010) "Why is SSR Important? A United Nations Perspective" in Mark Sedra (ed.) The Future of Security Sector Reform. The Centre for International Governance Innovation (CIGI), Waterloo, Ontario, Canada (www.cigionline.org)

Fayemi, K and Olonisakin, F (2010) "Nigeria" In Alan Bryden, Boubacar N'Diaye and 'Funmi Olonisakin (Eds.) Challenges of Security Sector Governance in West Africa. Geneva Centre for the Democratic Control of Armed Forces (DCAF): Geneva.

Goshit, Z.D. (2006). Economic, Politics and Ethno-Religious Relations in Jos Plateau Area During the Colonial Period (1900-1960).

Higazi, A (2008) "Social Mobilization and Collective Violence: Vigilantes and Militias in the Lowlands of Plateau State, Central Nigeria" in Pratten (ed), Journal of the International African Institute, (Special issue 'Perspectives on Vigilantism in Nigeria'). 78 (1):107-135, January 2008.

Human Right Watch (2001) Jos a City Torn Apart, Human Right Watch vol 13, No 9 (A) December 2001

Human Rights Watch (2005) Revenge in the Name of Religion: The cycle of Violence in Plateau and Kano States, Human Rights Watch, May 2005, Vol. 17, No. 8A

Human Rights Watch (2009) Arbitrary Killings by Security Forces Submission to the investigative Bodies on the November 20-29, 2008 Violence in Jos, Plateau state, Nigeria Human Rights watch, Newyork.

Hutton, L (2010) "Following the Yellow Brick Road? Current and Future Challenges for Security Sector Reform in Africa" in Mark Sedra (ed.) The Future of Security Sector Reform. The Centre for International Governance Innovation (CIGI), Waterloo, Ontario, Canada (www. cigionline.org)

Ostein, P (2009) Jonah Jang and the Jasawa; Ethno-Religious conflict in Jos Nigeria, Muslims –Christians Relations in Africa, August 2009.

Para-Mallam,O.J. ed. (2011) Finding Durable Peace in Plateau. National Institute Press: Kuru, Nigeria.

PIDAN, (2010) The History, Ownership and Establishment of Jos and Misconceptions about the Recurrent Jos Conflicts. Dan Sil Press. PIDAN

Pwajok, G.N.S. (2013) Policing in a Federal State: Whither Nigeria. Directorate of Research and Planning. Governor's Office, Jos.

Sedra, M. Ed. (2010) The Future of Security Sector Reform. The Centre for International Governance Innovation (CIGI), Waterloo, Ontario, Canada (www.cigionline.org)

Sha, D (1998): "Ethnicity and Political Conflicts In Jos: Emergence, Dimensions And The Way Forward". In Okoye Festus (ed), Ethnic and Religious Rights in Nigeria. Kaduna, HRM.

Newspapers

Adeleye, A. Jos Tragedy: Other Views Considered. Vanguard (Lagos) 28 January 2010, p.15.

Ali,V. That Jos Mayhem. Sunday Standard (Jos), 31 January 2010, p.5.

Agbese, A. Jos: Will Military Intervention stop Bloodshed? Cover Story. Weekly Trust September 17, 2011, p.6.

Agbese, A, and Mahmud,L. Jos: Sitting on a time bomb. Cover Story. Sunday Trust (Jos) 4 September 2011, p.7.

Ayuba,A. Police Transfers: A plot against Plateau State. The Nigeria Standard Friday, December 12, 2008.

Associated Press. Jos Crisis: New soldiers brought in. Tribune Newspapers on Line. Thursday 3 February 2011.

Jidauna, A. BYM condemns handling of Crisis. Sunday Standard (Jos), 31 January,2010 p.16

Newswatch (2010) "Jos Eruptsin Violence Again" Tuesday, 23rd January 2010.

Thisday (2010) Again, Plateau Burns, 22nd January 2010.

The Effects of Climate Change on the Herdsmen and Farmers Relationship in the North-Central Nigeria

By
Prof. Olayemi Akinwumi
NasarawaState University,
Keffi,
Department of History
yemiakinwumi@yahoo.com
234 0703 691 5955

Dr. Bilyaminu S. Muhammed,
Nasarawa State University,
Keffi,
Department of Sociology
bilyasule@nsuk.edu.ng
234 0803 335 2432

Dr. Theophilus. D. Lagi
Nasarawa State University,
Keffi,
Department of Sociology
teelagi@yahoo.com
234 0803 604 2488

Abstract

Climate change and Farmers- Fulani herdsmen conflict is of concern to governments and has generated serious scholarly attention in Nigeria. Statistics has shown that Nigeria has 22 million cows that consume about 1 billion gallons of water per day and 500 million kilograms of grass and forage crops. Desertification and drought caused by climate change in the far north coupled with the intensification of the Boko Haram crisis has caused Fulani herdsmen to abandon their foraging fields in the north east resulting in the migration southwards by the cattle herders. The increased southward movement of the Fulani herdsmen led to conflicts with local communities resulting to loss of life and property; seriously affected inter-group relations and corporate existence of the country. This paper examines the effect of climate change and the crisis in North Central Nigeria, and the increasing conflicts between host farming communities and Fulani herdsmen and its impact on inter-group relations in North Central Nigeria. The paper relied on data from secondary sources such as books, journals, conference papers, reports from national sources and international organizations and it is basically descriptive. The paper finds that climate change is a serious threat to the socio-economic activities of the Fulani herdsmen in Northern Nigeria. Furthermore, the Fulani herdsmen are forced to migrate to other states with favourable climatic conditions. They are viewed as threats and this lead to conflicts between the host communities and the Fulani herdsmen leading to loss of lives and properties and serious effect on intergroup relations. The paper recommends the creation of large acres of ranches across the country which should be allotted to the Fulani herdsmen; the government should sensitize and educate the host communities and the Fulani herdsmen on the need for ranching and peaceful co-habitation and national integration.

Key Words: Climate Change, Herdsmen Farmers Relationship, Intergroup Relationship

Introduction

The world has been experiencing changes in its physical environment. Rapid population increase and climate change has impacted on its environmental sustainability. It is not an exaggeration that nations within the global system are facing multi-dimensional challenges associated with endemic conflicts and wars. According to Alao (2015) African, Asia, and the Middle East were and still are the hot spots of conflicts and wars involving militias and separatists groups. Africa had 26 conflicts involving 162 militias and separatists groups in Central African Republic (CAR) and south Sudan (civil war), Democratic Republic of Congo, Sudan and South Sudan (war against Rebel); Mali, Somalia, Nigeria, Chad, Niger and Cameroon (Islamic Separatist-Boko Haram). While the Middle East had 8 conflicts involving 180 militias and separatists groups in Israel, Iran, Lebanon, Syria, Yemen, Palestine. In Asia, there were 17 conflicts involving 133 militias and separatists group in Afghanistan, Philippines and Pakistan (Islamists), Burma-Myamar (war against rebels) and Thailand. The regions with less conflicts are America with 5 number of conflicts involving 25 militias and separatists group in Mexico and Colombia (Drug cartels); Europe with 16 conflicts involving 71 militias and separatists group in Chechnya and Dagestan (Islamists), Ukraine and Luhank (Secession) (Alao, 2015 p1).

The nature of conflicts in Africa is rooted in Islamic separatist insurgency, ethnic and communal conflicts, natural resource control agitations and political violence. For instance, Egypt between January 25, 2011 to 2014, there was Egyptian revolution which was political that overthrow Hosni Mubarak government, the November 22, 2012 to July 3, 2013 Egyptian protests, June 28, 2013 – July 3, 2013 protests, July 3, 2013 to 2014 political violence. On February 23, 2011 to 2014, there was the Sinai insurgency. Conflicts in Sudan took the dimension of war, ethnic violence and insurgency. These conflicts include 1987 to 2014 Lord's Resistance army insurgency, 2003 to 2014 war in Darfur, December 18, 2005 to January 15, 2010 Chad-Sudan conflict, May 26, 2009 to 2014 Sudanese nomadic conflicts, January 7, 2011 to 2014 ethnic violence in South Sudan and May 19, 2011 to 2014 Sudan SRF conflict. In South Sudan between March 26, 2012 to September 26, 2012, there was Sudan South Sudan border war and the South Sudanese civil war from December 15, 2013 to 2014. Since 2011, Libya has been experiencing militia violent conflicts with various militias groups holding forth the regions in the country. Somalia since January 26, 1991 to 2014 experienced Somalia civil war and continued violence by Islamist group El-Shabab. In Mali, there was April 11, 2002 to 2014. Insurgency in the Maghreb, 2007 – 2009 second Tuareg rebellion, 2012 third Tuareg rebellion and 2012 to 2014 Northern Mali conflict. Niger on its part had April 11, 2002 – 2014 insurgency in the Maghreb, 2007 to 2009 second Azawad insurgency, 2012 Tuareg rebellion and The Central African Republic (CAR) had the 1987 – 2014 Lord's Resistance Army insurgency, 2004 to 2007 Central African Republic Bush War and the 2012 to 2014 Central African Republic Conflict 2012 – 2014. Since 2009 Nigeria has been having pockets of Boko Haram insurgents' attacks on cities and villages in the Northeast as well as neighboring villages in Cameroun, Niger and Chad respectively. Since the inception of the Buhari administration in May, 2015, the Fulani herdsmen and farmers conflict has been intensified especially in the North Central states of Nigeria.

These conflicts have lead to a steady growth in the number of people displaced and refugee like situation between 2008 and 2014. In Africa, statistics from UNHCR (2014) revealed that the number of refugees was put at nearly 3.4 million, while internally displaced persons (IDPs) stood at 5.4 million. In Nigeria, the Boko Haram insurgencies since 1999 has displaced over 2 million people in the North East and thousands are killed, as well as property worth millions was destroyed. Since the degradation of the Boko Haram insurgents in December, 2015, the country is experiencing another wave of violent conflicts by the Fulani herdsmen. The current Fulani herdsmen militia in 2013 did not rank among the top five groups, having caused the death of only 63 people. The following year, however, the group militants were responsible for 1,229 deaths, which placed them at number four on the list of terrorist, out done by only the Taliban, the Islamic State and Boko Haram (Burton, 2017). In the first quota of 2016, the Fulani herdsmen militia was responsible for nearly 500 deaths and has showed no signs of slowing down. According to Burton (2017) it has been predicted that the Fulani herdsmen might well surpass Boko Haram as Nigeria's most dangerous group. The continued killing and destruction by Fulani herdsmen in some parts of Nigeria has led to the extent that opinion leaders and poor citizens in the country are calling for the government to declare them terrorist group like the Boko Haram and Indigenous People of Biafra (IPOB).

The current Fulani herdsmen and Farmers conflict and their neighbours stem from a long history of feuding, farming and herding. Pre-existing communal conflicts have fueled violence as herdsmen turn militants in the face of urbanization, desertification and indifference of the Nigerian governments to their plight. The herdsmen have engaged in conflict with farmers in North Central states of Benue, Plateau, Nasarawa, Niger, Kogi and Taraba, Adamawa states in the North East, Kaduna, Zamfara states in the North West, as well some states in the South East and South West regions. The conflict is as a result of the struggle for grazing land and access to drinking water for the cattle and humans. The conflict between herdsmen and farmers is eclectic, in some cases it is political, ethnic, religious, resource control or a combination of these factors. The Fulani herdsmen have simpler goals, being herders, their attacks though sometimes in retribution for the death of kinsmen or meant to target rival communities, are focused on gaining graze able land for their cattle. While their Islamic faith often sets them at odds with local communities. They target civilians largely focusing on clearing land and inflicting casualties through the use of firearms Burton, 2017). Pressure from population increase, urbanization and desertification as a result of climate change and indifference of the Nigerian government has contributed the violence and insecurity in the affected states.

There is no doubt that Nigeria's population is increasing rapidly from 88.5 million people in 1991 and 140 million people in 2006 to over 180 million in 2017. The United Nations in 2013 predicted that Africa and Nigeria in particular will be at the forefront of huge global population size over the next century (Bilyaminu, 2015). Not only that the country's population is increasing, climate change has resulted in various environmental challenges such as flooding which devastated Benue, Nasarawa, Kogi and Lagos states in 2012 and reoccurring in 2013, 2014, 2016 and 2017. Climate change as a phenomenon touches very much on many sectors such as agriculture, environment and survival of human beings. The most common feature of climate change is global warming (Okolo, 2010). The global warming as a result of climate change has affected the average weather of a region or the earth resulting in changes in average temperature, amount of rainfall, sunshine and desertification. The cause of climate change was often thought to be natural and not easily identifiable. But this perception has changed. Today's changes in the climate are increasingly brought about by human activities (IPCC, 2007).

According to the IPCC report of 2007, those who are already the most vulnerable and marginalized that experience the greatest impacts of climate change. Land use by the large population include deforestation leading to desertification, human development of the landscape for agricultural activities, road and building construction, dumping of solid waste and burning of waste affect and change the environment by changing the amount of water going into and out of a place; influence the ground cover and change the quantity of sunlight that is absorbed, climate change also leads to experiencing of sea and river floods, which is as a result of warmer temperature particularly in the Northern parts of Nigeria. This threatens the biodiversity such as plants and animals' population, rivers and lakes, protected covers and habitats (Okolo, 2010). Thus, the effects of climate change in Nigeria have increasingly resulted in the incessant conflict between herdsmen and farmers. This conflict threatened the corporate existence of Nigeria, the relationship between the farmers and herdsmen which used to be symbiotic desertification and drought caused by climate change in the far North coupled with the intensification of the Boko Haram insurgency. In a report by Ejike Chukwu in *Nigeria Today* of 8th April, 2018, cited Shehu Kyari Ibn Umar El-Kanemi, the Shehu of Bama while speaking at an Educational Foundation in Etekwuru, Egbema in Ohaji of Imo state, noted that the federal government failed to take action when Boko Haram sect was still in its incubating stage, rather allowed the sect to expand and eventually became a problem to the Nigerian society. He noted that Boko Haram is a creation of the federal government because the government at that time did not take them serious due to the fact that, at that time, the government of the day did not come in to arrest the situation at the beginning of the uprising. Thus, the Boko Haram insurgents became a law into themselves. The Boko Haram sect are still around, rampaging and attacking soft targets in Maiduguri and its environs where a number of people died even though they have been degraded according to the Military and the Federal Government, they need to be mopped up. Climate change and the Boko Haram insurgency has caused the Fulani herdsmen to abandon their foraging fields in the North East resulting in their migration Southwards to the North Central states and other parts of Nigeria. The increased movement southwards of the Fulani herdsmen led to conflicts with local communities who are mostly farmers and seriously affected inter group relations between the Fulani herdsmen and the local communities in the affected states in the North Central Nigeria.

Literature Review

Climate change as a phenomenon touches very much on many sectors such as agriculture, environment and survival of human beings. The most common feature of climate change is global warming (Okolo, 2010). The global warming as a result of climate change has affected the average weather of a region or the earth resulting in changes in average temperature, amount of rainfall, sunshine and desertification. The cause of climate change was often thought to be natural and not easily identifiable. But this perception has changed because today's changes in the climate are increasingly brought about by human activities (IPCC, 2007). According to the IPCC report of 2007, those who are already the most vulnerable and marginalized are those that experience the greatest impacts of climate change.

According to Okolo (2010) climate change is a relatively a new phenomenon to many people in the sense that it is being recently understood. Climate change as a phenomenon touches very much on many sectors such as agriculture, environment and survival of human beings. Climate change has been observed to have global and complex environmental challenges. The most common feature of climate change is global warming. Okolo (2010) defined climate change as a long-term significant change in the average weather of a region or the earth. Factors responsible for climate change include changes in average temperature, amount of rainfall, days of sunshine. It also has elements of changes in external factors that shape climate such as solar radiation, earth orbit, as well as human (anthropogenic activities). Climate change occurs after a much extended period of time. The cause of climate change was often thought to be natural and not easily identifiable. But this perception has changed; today changes in the climate are increasingly brought about by human activities. IPPC (2007) cited by Okolo (2010) noted that in the past 100 year, the World's surface air temperature has warmed up by an average of 0.6^0C. This may not sound alarming, but it has effect already on the world.

The former United nations Secretary-General, Banki-Moon cited in Okolo (2010) has described climate change as the greatest challenge facing a world beset by crisis. The international debate on climate change has recently gained momentum with particular concern for the implications in Africa. Africa is already vulnerable and will become more so (Brito and Bosquet, 2005 cited by Bilyaminu, 2015). Africa and indeed Nigeria, is already more exposed to natural disasters such as flooding in cities and villages and the ensuing human and environmental problems such as vector-borne diseases, crop failures and transformation of ecosystems being more pronounced. Also, Okolo (2010) noted that the Academic of Sciences in 2001 report affirmed that climate change has been part of the earth's 4.6 billion year history. Climate change as earlier mentioned is brought about by many process as a result of natural or human causes. The National Academy of Sciences reported that human activities, particularly in the last 100 years have significantly altered the energy balance of the earth, the growing population, as well as increasing demand for energy and land resources. The natural events that cause climate change include greenhouse gas (GHG) concentration, solar radiation orbital variation, volcanic emption, ocean variability and glaciations. The human activities on the other hand include pollution of the atmosphere by uncontrolled industrial processes environmental pollution leading to the build-up of greenhouse gases that result in global warming. Human population growth has led to increasing demand for energy and land resources. As a result, human have been altering the earth's energy balance through many ways which include the burning of fossil fuels to produce energy for various uses, and through land use change for agriculture and forest production. The main human activities identified to cause climate change include fossil fuel combustion, sulphateaerosols and black carbon production, cement manufacture, land use activities and livestock production activities. The Guardian (2008) estimated that fossil fuel have increased carbon (IV) oxide levels from 280ppm to 387ppm and estimated that the concentration are increasing at a rate of 2-3ppm/year. Scientists have projected that if the current rates of emission of carbon (IV) oxide continue, its concentration will reach a range of 535 to 983ppm by the end of 21st century. Along with rising methane levels, these changes are expected to cause an increase in temperature of 1.4-5.6^0C between 1990 and 2100 (Okolo, 2010). According to Ruddiman (2001) cited by Bilyaminu (2015) of most concern in these anthropogenic factors is the increase in CO_2 levels due to emissions from fossil fuel or combustion, followed by aerosols (particulate matter in the atmosphere) and the CO_2 released by cement and other manufactures. Other factors, including land use, ozone depletion, animal agriculture and deforestation, are also of concern in the roles they play – both separately and in conjunction with other factors – in affecting climate, and measures of climate variables.

The effect of ecological disaster in the Lake Chad basin poses serious problem of insecurity between pastoralists and farmer in the region and the middle belt. Over 40 million people across Nigeria, Chad, Cameroun, Niger and the Central Republic depend on water from the Chad basin for survival. The Lake has shrunk overtime and desertification has intensified over the years, large numbers of people, once dependent on the Lake for livelihood like fishing, irrigation for dry season farming, drinking water for cattle, have been left bereft. Migration and resettlement have intensified, farmers and fishermen have been confronted with leaner harvest, and pastoralist has been compelled to venture to other locations in search of food and water for their cattle. That foray deeper southwards has lead to deadly clashes between herdsmen and farmer in different states in Nigeria, and it is not surprising to note that, the North East of Nigeria and the far west of Chad where the lake is situated have in the past years been the epicenter of Boko Haram insurgency.

Climate change increase atmospheric temperature depletion of the ozone layer (that is the gas shield that protects the earth's surface from the sun), increase in ocean temperature. Increasing ocean and sea temperature are resulting in severe bleaching and an increase in the death of the world's coral reefs. More ocean, sea and river floods are also being experienced as a result of warmer temperature which cause evaporation and lead to heavier rain falls in some regions including Nigeria. Climate change also cause rising sea level, ocean acidification, heat waves, and threat to biodiversity such as plant/animals population rivers/lakes, protected covers and habitats. Action related to climate change is however, part of comprehensive issue of sustainable urban development. Therefore, climate change has to be considered at every stage for integrated urban development (Wiebusch, 2012 cited by Bilyaminu, 2015). Land use activities that affect climate change include irrigation, deforestation, agricultural activities, road and building construction, dumping of solid waste and burning of waste. They essentially affect and change the environment by changing the amount of water going into and out of a place; influence the ground cover and change the quantity of sunlight that is absorbed. Deforestation can lead to desertification. More recently, temperatures in some cities have risen, with much higher increase in urban areas due to extensive human development of the landscape.

To demonstrate the impact of climate change in Nigeria, NEMA in 2010 gave statistics of disasters in Nigeria. It reported that disasters claimed the lives of 1,555 persons, while 258,000 were displaced in various flood disasters in different parts of the country. The flood disasters also brought with it epidemics such as cholera arising from contaminated waters, with about 20,600 cases reported in 17 states by heath authorities. The 2010 flood and subsequent years have rendered thousands homeless and in addition, loss of hectres of farmlands with various crops among others. For instance, NEMA reported that in 2010, floods devastated over 100 villages in Sokoto state and over 23,700 households were rendered homeless in addition to the loss of 32,853 hectres of farmlands with various crops. These communities in addition, had lost almost all their cumulative savings, grains storage and faced livelihood challenges. Environmental sustainability has become increasingly used by international donor agencies such as the World Bank, United Nations and other donor agencies including governments. Since the 1992 Rio Earth Summit there has been serious concern on conserving the environmental resources to sustain this generation and future generations. The thinking is also to the global economy greener especially in terms of energy use and reversed global climate emissions. However, the advisory council on global change (WBGU) recons that the challenge is hug and that the trend in global carbon emissions needs to be reversed by 2020 at the latest otherwise, the risks of climate change will spin out of control (Boschert and Pilardeaux, 2011 cited in Bilyaminu, 2015). Environmental sustainability focuses on conditions of safeguarding the world's natural life support system. According to Baker (2006) the term 'sustainability' originally belongs to ecology, and it referred to the potential of the ecosystem to subsist overtime. The rise of global environmental problems, such as climate change, biodiversity loss and deforestation, growing energy needs in both developing and newly industrializing countries and growing population in the world has led to a growing demand for international interventions to deal with both transboundary and global environmental matters.

The UN Conference on environment and development (UNCED) in Rio de Janeiro in 1992 was supposed to be a mile stone in environmental policy. According to Bilyaminu (2015) citing Unmussig (2012) noted one thing has changed since Rio 1992 with investments in more efficient technologies and renewable energies are increasing. This is a fact because there has been increasing investment and awareness on economy friendly innovations and investment and products are green and eco friendly known as the green economy which is one of the topics for Rio+ 20, the follow up to the 1992 conference in June 2012. From African perspective, Donal Kaberuka, the president of the African Development Bank (AFDB) in 2012 Conference on Development and environment in Johanesburg, observed that due to annual growth rates of around six per cent, many African countries have progressed in recent years. However, experts have agreed that more needs to be done to stem poverty in the long run, because as population keep growing fast and global warming is likely to erase some of the recent achievements. He further estimated that 100 million more people w2ill drop into poverty unless climate change is halted. He argued that Africa is not a poor continent and that it is rich in natural resources, and the commodity sector has been growing fast. The AFDB president appreciated the idea of a 'green economy' – a way of doing business that is geared to environmental sustainability, profitability and social inclusion.

The Federal Government national report in 2012 noted that Nigeria was an active participant at the Riot 20 Conference. In particular, the government of Nigeria took serious cognizance of the imperative to address issues of climate change in the context of sustainable development. This will include support to local authorities, increasing public awareness and enhancing participation of urban residents, including the poor in decision making; promoting, protecting and restoring safe and green urban spaces; safe and clean drinking water and sanitation, healthy air quality, generation of decent jobs, and improved urban planning and slum upgrading, supporting sustainable management of waste through the application of the 3Rs (reduce, revise and recycle); mainstreaming disaster risk reduction, resilience and climate risks in urban planning; and promoting sustainable development policies that support inclusive housing and social services; a safe and healthy living environment for all, particularly children, youth, women and the elderly and disabled; affordable and sustainable transport and energy . Similarly, Federal Government in 2012 observed that Nigeria is reach in natural resources like minerals, fossil fuels, biodiversity and forests and so on. The environment and natural resources provides environmental protection, goods and services to communities and provision of pharmaceuticals and sustainable tourism. Sustainable ways to exploit environmental goods and services as well as to protect it should be the drive towards a green economy (Bilyaminu, 2015). Green economy is an economy that results in improved human well-being and social equity, while significantly reducing environmental risks and ecological scarcities.

The survival of man depends largely on the availability and wise use of the endowments of what nature has given him- the environment which harbours the resources he needs such as land, water and forest resources. The exploitation of these resources must however be done in a manner that guarantees safety for the present while also providing for the future. While there are natural ways of replenishing the earth's resources, human activities can also support the regeneration of these resources to make them sustainable if they are conducted in the most appropriate way. Land use by the large population include deforestation leading to desertification, human development of the landscape for agricultural activities, road and building construction, dumping of solid waste and burning of waste affect and change the environment by changing the amount of water going into and out of a place; influence the ground cover and change the quantity of sunlight that is absorbed, climate change also leads to experiencing of sea and river floods, which is as a result of warmer temperature particularly in the Northern parts of Nigeria.

As countries around the world continue to advance economically, they put a strain on the ability of the natural environment to absorb the high level of pollutants that are created as a part of this economic growth. To ensure sustainability, solutions need to be found so that the economies of the world can continue to grow, but not at the expense of the public good. In the world of economics, the amount of environmental quality must be considered as limited in supply and therefore must be treated as a scarce resource (Dresner, 2002). This is a resource that must be protected to ensure its sustainability. The ability of society to improve the wellbeing of its citizens offers them the opportunity to raise their capacity to engage in productive activities in a sustainable way which is one way of attaining the global objective of economic growth and its sustainability. This ensures the reduction in the poverty rates of these nations which entails improvement in the rate of deprivation of the individuals' ability to undertake his social and economic activities without hindrance compared to that of another. It also means bridging the gap between the extremely rich and the poor in society, reduction in the dependency ratio which ensures that development is sustainable; this is where a larger proportion of the population becomes self-reliant (Ichoku, 2005).

Our environment affects our lives and our relationships as humans in a community or as ethnic group. The quality of the environment in which a person lives, is thus, inextricably linked with the quality of life he or she enjoys especially through his/her socio-economic status. Man's seemingly unlimited power to dominate his environment and exploit the natural resources therein for selfish reasons, needs and desires has obscured his appreciation of the fact that he or she is but one unit. A part of the comprehensive system of dynamic inter-dependencies that is more than the sum of its parts'. Thus, human activities may affect the environment while many factors in the environment may also have negative or positive impact on people's welfare. Living beings are dependent upon their physical environment- the land, water, air and energy for their existence (Nettle, 2009). At the same time they also affect the physical components just as the changed physical conditions again have a direct impact on living beings. Human activities which affect the environment causing it to be hostile or less compatible to man are responsible for changing patterns of the climate. According to the (United Nations, 2014) man's actions poses the greatest danger to a sustainable future through over-exploitation of the earth's resources or unsafe disposal of wastes in a manner that harms the ecosystem. The total environment specifically includes not just the biosphere of earth, air, and water, but also human interactions with these things, with nature, and what humans have created as their surroundings.

There is no doubt that clean and accessible water is an essential need for all peoples in any part of the world to enable them function properly and have a healthy life. The herdsmen and their live stalks require huge amount of water for their survival and that of the animals. Though there is sufficient fresh water on earths planet to achieve this however, bad economics or poor infrastructure is hindering the achievement of this goal leading to the death of millions of people and lives talks associated with inadequate water supply. Added to this, is the fact that water scarcity and its quality and inadequate sanitation negatively impact on food security of nations. Drought has become even more threatening affecting most of the world's poor countries including Nigeria, worsening already the current hunger situation and malnutrition. In other areas, floods have become more pronounced in the last decade and half bringing in its wake disasters which account for 70 per cent of deaths related to natural disasters (World Meteorological Agency, 2015). Worldwide, insufficient water quality and supply, sanitation and hygiene are believed to be the second biggest cause, after malnutrition, of loss of potentially healthy years of life (Ljubin-Sternak&Tomislav, 2014). These are years which if available to man will enable him to be productive raising the general level of his welfare and the environment. Poor water quality is worst in rural areas of North Central Nigeria. Nasarawa State one of the herders and farmers crisis state only 2 per cent of the population can access portable water even at an enormous cost (FMH, 2015).The linkage between water supply, farming and grazing is important. The picture above paint a grim picture of what a battered environment as a result of climate can be especially where man's actions are uncontrolled in managing it. These actions which have created extreme weather condition have led to the phenomenon of climate change which currently affects the world and the North Central part of Nigeria with its attendant negative impact on resource availability and utilization as well as persistent conflict between herders and farmers resulting in stain relationship among them at the communal level and the nation at large.

Theoretical Framework

The paper adopts the conflict theory to have understanding of the Fulani herdsmen and farmers conflict using the various school thoughts and views. The issue of contemporary conflict at all levels of society is explained by conflict scholars such as Karl Marx (1813-1883), Dahrendorf (1958) and Marx Weber. According to Udo and Adoyi (2016) Karl Marx views that the more the rate or degree of inequality in thedistribution of the relatively available scarce resources in the society, the greater is the basic conflict of interest between its dominant and subordinate segments. Marx opined that the degree of inequality in the distribution of the resources generates inherent conflicts of interest. The lack of equity in the distribution of the resources and dominance of one group over the other, the more the subordinate segments became aware of their collective interests; the more likely they are to question the legitimacy of the existing pattern of distribution or allocation of resources. Marx also asserted that the more the subordinates segments in a system become aware of their collective interests and questioned the legitimacy of the distribution of scarce resources; the more likely they are to join in overt conflict against dominant segments of a system.

Udo& Adoyi (2016) noted that Darhendorf (1958) viewed of conflict as productive and constructive. He saw conflict as necessary for achieving an end in the society or for the realization of social goals. Darhendorf attempt to determine a systematic locus and a specific framework for a theory of conflict in Sociological analysis. He contended that there are two different kinds of struggles in an organization conflict (exogenous and endogenous conflicts). The endogenous conflict is generated within an organization, system or a society. He agreed with Marx that conflict comes from the present social structure. The theory asserted that certain conflicts are based on certain social structural arrangements and hence are bound to arise whenever such structural arrangements are given. Darhendorf presented some assumptions for the structural arrangement which could lead to conflict in his conflict model. They include; in every imperatively coordinated group, the carriers of positive (statusquo) and the negative (change of status quo) dominant roles determine two quasi-groups with opposite latent interest; the bearers of positive and negative dominant roles organize themselves into groups with manifest interests unless certain empirically variable conditions intervene; interest groups which originate in this manner are in constant conflict concerned with the preservation or changew in the status quo; the conflict among interest groups in the sense of this model leads to changes in the structure of the social relations in question through changes in the dominant relations.

The situation in Nigeria is that there are unequal distribution of resources particularly land for grazing for the Fulani herdsmen. The lands were either allocated for developmental projects by governments to construction companies, individuals and organizations. Moreso, the population pressure as a result of rapid population growth and urbanization in the country has affected land distribution and uses, coupled with effect of climate change leading to uneven rainfall and desertification. The Fulani herdsmen have limited grazing land and water which their animals compete with humans, as well as cultivation of farms along their routes or tracks. The dominance of the larger population on the available resources as against the small community of Fulani herdsmen has resulted in tension and conflicts. The Fulani herdsmen have simpler goals of focusing on gaining their grazing land for their cattle. That's why immediately the anti-grazing law was enacted late last year in Benue state, it generated more conflict between the people (farmers) and the herdsmen. The Fulani herdsmen became aware that the law has deprived of them of their rights of open grazing or collective interest. The continuous conflict in Benue state is questioning the legitimacy of Benue state government by extension Taraba state, neighbouring state on the legitimacy of regulating the distribution of the scarce resources which was free for all. The Fulani herdsmen vow to fight for their right and thus join in overt conflict against the dominant segments of the societies in the North Central states of Nigeria.

Sources of Data

The paper utilized secondary data from books, journals, and internet, national and international sources among others. The paper is basically descriptive.

Fulani Herdsmen and Farmers Crisis in Nigeria

The Fulani herdsmen have been part of Nigeria's population for centuries. Naij. Com (2018) traced the history of Fulani herdsmen in Nigeria and today's crisis. It noted that Fulani (Fula) are nomadic people. The Fulani (Fulbe) are inhabited in many countries of Western Africa, but most of them are concentrated in the North of Nigeria and Senegal. Anthropologists pointed that the origin of Fula is connected with Egypt. They were called gypsies descendants or sons of Roman legionaries lost in the Sahara. Some others even hypothesize that Fulani is one of the Israel tribes. Others believed that Fula originated from the region of present Northern Senegal. Gradually, a century after century they migrated with their herds in West Africa savannas occupying new territories. They mingled with Berbers of Northern Africa and other nomadic Sahara tribes. The Fula was divided into a large number of groups with different names including Fulbe, Gourma, Fellata, Fula, Bororos, Voda, Peul and Pular. But all of them are distinguished by a noble appearance, proud posture and a lighter skin. The Fulani herdsmen are largely located in the Sahel and semi arid parts of West Africa but due to climate change or changes in climate patterns, many herdsmen have moved further south into savannah and tropical forest belt of West Africa in Nigeria, Niger, Senegal, Guinea, Mauritania, Mali, Burkina Faso, Ghana, Benin, Cote d'Ivoire and Cameroon. Cattle are the dominant composition of the Fulani herd in Nigeria. Fulani herdsmen engage in both random and planned transhumance movements. Transhumance is a type of nomadism or pastoralism, a seasonal movement of people with their livestock between fixed summer and winter pastures.

In Nigeria, the livestock supplied the herdsmen provide a bulk of the beef consumption in the country. Modern Fulani are divided into nomadic pastoralists, semi-nomadic, and sedentary. The sedentary or settled Fulani are mixed with neighbouring peoples. A lot of them are under the influence of the Hausa agricultural people. The Fulani herdsmen who are pastoralist engage in grazing and managing the herds. They began to engage in cattle breeding since the 13th to 14th century. The task is carried out by the men who find grazing sites, build tents and camps and make security tools such as knives, bow and arrows and den guns. While the women take on the traditional roles of milking the cows, weaving and mat making and sourcing food produce in the market. Some women are also involved in faming and raising poultry (Iro, 1994). This traditional culture is preserved by the Fulani nomads. In Nigeria today the Fulani herdsmen engage in exchange of livestock products for agricultural products, famous in as professional shepherds and they take farmers' livestock for grazing in exchange for offspring and farming products (naija.ng, 2018). This therefore, shows a symbiotic relationship between Fulani herdsmen and farmers in Nigeria. During the centuries of their relationship, Fulani herdsmen (nomads) and farmers often come to conflict. In the past, the nomads have conflicts with local farmers emanating from the herdsmen cattle eating up farmers produce in the farm or some forms trespass which are usually settled by the traditional rulers or in the law courts. Recently, the nature of the conflict and attacks have changed to the extent that the news reports from the daily newspapers in Nigeria reports that Fulani herdsmen now allegedly use firearms to attack local communities and farmers in the north central states of Benue (Logo and Gwer local government areas), Plateau (Barikin Ladi, Bokkos, Riyom and Bassa local government areas) Nasarawa Nasrawa Eggon, Awe, Obi and Keana local government areas), Kogi, and Taraba, Adamawa in the North east as well as Kaduna, Zamfara in the North West states in the South east and South west.

In 2017, the Fulani herders- farmers' conflict became more pronounced with the constant attacks in Southern Kaduna communities and border communities in Nasarawa and Benue states. Dailypost.ng of April 24, 2018 (online) noted that an early morning attack by suspected herdsmen at Ayar Mbalom village in Gwer East local government area of Benue state led to the killing of 19 persons and over 35 houses burnt. In a similar attack reported by Don Silas in the Daily Post of April 23, 2018, there wass violent attack on Kpanche community in Bassa local government areas of Kogi state by Fulani herdsmen. The death toll reached 16 from 12 persons, and some houses were set on fire. However, John Akinfehinwa on April 22, 2018, in his report for Daily post, noted that the incidence may not be unconnected with the December, 2016 crisis between Igburra Mozun people and Bassa Kwomus, when the former (Igburra Mozun) people attached the masquerade of the Bassa Kwomus. The incidence led to the displacement of Igburra people (Daily Post, 23 April, 2018 online, retrieved on 25/4/2018 at 12.00pm). In continuing wave of attacks, some gunmen have invaded some Churches in Benue state killing the Priests and some followers on April 26, 2018, Ewubare (2018) reported that gunmen have invaded a Church in Logo Local Government Area of Benue State, killing seven people. In another attack on 24th April, 2018, gunmen had invaded a Catholic Church in Gwer West Local Government Area of the state. The gunmen reportedly shot two priests and 17 Church members. Of course, the gunmen are said to be herdsmen who are unleashing violent attacks in the state since the establishment of the anti-grazing law.

Similarly, in Plateau state, in January 24, 2018 at Josho village in Daffo district of Bokkos was raised in a communal class. Ameh Godwin of Daily Post (2018) cited the News Agency of Nigeria (NAN) report that said a woman and two men were killed and several others were injured in the fracas. According to him, an insider gave an insight into the fracas which resulted from an alleged encroachment into the land of some natives by a herdsman, who was moulding much blocks to build a house. It further noted that; it started like a simple disagreement, which was thought it was a very simple misunderstanding that could be settled, but it soon turned bloody, leaching to the death of three people (NAN source, 2018). Simon Angyol, chairman, interim management Committee of Bokkos local government confirmed the clash and corroborated the earlier assertions that the incident resulted from a "very simple disagreement over land encroachment". The Nigeria Police, Plateau State Command also confirmed the incident where the entire village had been razed down. In the same vein, Godwin reported for dailypost.ng of April, 19 2018, pointed out that gunmen killed four construction workers at Angwan-Rogo village in Jebu-Miango area of Bassa local government area, Plateau State. The workers were fetching sand for an ongoing construction work, when the gunmen attacked them. The Police Comand in Plateau State, confirmed the attack and that four persons were killed by the gunmen. Those killed were confirmed to be men who are labourers excavating sand for their construction work. Typer, the Police public relation officer in the state, claimed that the attackers were herdsmen (Dailypost online, 19 April, 2018). Again, the Daily Post of 9th April, 2018 reported that the killings in Plateau communities have continued unabated. Eight people were said to have been killed by suspected herdsmen in Nding Loh, Fan District of Barkin Ladi Local Government Area, Plateau State. The incident according to Daily Post reporter Agabus Pwanagba occurred at a relaxation centre on Sunday evening within the entrance of the community. Pwanagba noted that the community had been under threat of attack in recent times. The attack resulted on the death of seven people (Daily Post, 2018). However, Terna, the Plateau

Police Command public relation officer argued that 5 persons died immediately after the incident and that two out of the three injured victims taken to the Plateau Specialist Hospitals, Jos died.

Nurudeen (2018) reporting in Naij.com noted that the herders-farmers clashes in Nigeria have worsened in recent years and are spreading southward, threatening the county's security and stability. The clashes have become potentially dangerous as Boko Haram insurgency in the northeast. Furthermore, Nurudeen (2018) provided nine facts about the herders-farmers conflicts in Nigeria. He pointed that the herders-farmers conflict or clashes can be situated in the context of other ethnic conflicts, attributed to actors primarily divided along fault lines of cultural, ethnic or religious communities and identities; herder- farmer conflicts usually involve dispute over land and or cattle between herders in particular, the Fulani and farmers, in particular, the Tiv or Berom or communities in Josho in Daffo district of Bokkos local government area of Plateau state and Alago in Keana and Awe local government areas of Nasarawa state. Third, accusation over cattle rustling and farmland grazing spark conflict. In some States in the North West such as Nasarawa, Zamfara and Birnin Gwari local government area of Kaduna state, at the heart of the conflict are rustling and clashes over grazing on farmlands in Nasarawa, Benue, and some parts of South east and south west states. These often pitch the farmers in violent conflicts with the herders. Herders also accuse natives along grazing routes of stealing their cows and this leads to clashes. Fouth, is the issue of climate change which has devastating consequences for the herders in the far northern states, with its effect on rainfall affecting water reserves and fodders for animal feeds. Since the return of civil rule in Nigeria in 1999, farmers- herders' conflict and violence has contributed to loss of thousands of lives and destruction several properties worth millions or billions of Naira. It also displaced tens of thousands of people from their communities and villages. Nurdeen (2018) observed that it followed a trend in the increase of farmer-herder conflicts throughout much of the western Sahel, due to an expansion of agriculturist population and cultivated land at the expense of pastureland; deteriorating environmental condition. Moreso, climate change has led to shift south ward of the Sahara desert resulting in the desertification and soil degradation in some parts of Nigeria. This has resulted in the Fulani herdsmen increase movement south wards in search of food and water for themselves and their cattle thereby leading to conflict and clashes in the states of the North central Nigeria. Fifth, apart from climate change, since the founding of Nigeria's fourth republic in 1999, the country has been experiencing communal, ethnic, religious, political agitations and economic crisis resulting from massive corruption and economic sabotage. These leads to breakdown of law and order, insecurity and violence. Insecurity and insurgency by Boko Haram sect in the Northeast Nigeria have led many populations to create self-defense forces, ethnic militias, state run militias, armed gangs, vigilante groups which have been used to engage in further violence. Reports from newspapers in Nigeria indicated that leaders of state armed guards were arrested as perpetrators of the herders-farmers conflict. For example in Benue state it was reported that one Yamini, a leader of the anti-grazing law was arrested by the military as a master mind of some of the attacks in the state and he was alleged to be a member of Boko Haram sect. The same scenario played out in Taraba state where some youth said to be government sponsored militias were arrested by the military for unleashing violence in the name of Fulani herdsmen. The crisis is now taking a new dimension with religion brought to bear, particularly in Benue conflict. The majority of farmer-herder clashes have occurred between Muslim Fulani herdsmen and Christian peasants, coupled with the killings of two catholic pastors in Benue state. This has exacerbated ethno religious hostilities in some communities in Benue and plateau state. Christian Association of Nigeria and Catholic church has accused the federal government of religious bias.

The President, Muhammadu Buhari on 10th April, 2018 in London while being a guest to Archbishop of Canterbury, Justin Welby, recounted that the herdsmen and farmers clashes in Nigeria is even older than us. It has always been there but now made worse by the influx of armed gunmen from the Sahel region into different parts of the West African sub region. These gunmen were trained and armed by Muammar Gadaffi of Libya. When he was killed, the gunmen escaped with their arms. We encountered some of them fighting with Boko Haram. Herdsmen we used to know carried only sticks and may be a cutlass to clear the way, but these ones now carry sophisticated weapons. The problem is not religious, but sociological and economic (Adesina, 2018). He further noted that irresponsible politics has been brought into the farmers/herders crisis and assured for an enduring solutions and justice to the crisis.

The Federal Government who bear the brunt of these herders- farmers conflict have proposed a number of measures which includes ranching, cattle colonies and grazing routes. Ewubare (2018) reported in naija online that the federal government has banned the movement of herdsmen in Benue, Taraba, Adamawa, Kaduna and Plateau states. This was a decision reached at the National Economic Council (NEC) held on 26th April, 2018 chaired by the Vice President of Nigeria, Yemi Osinbajo, comprising of the 36 state Governors and relevant ministries of government and the Central Bank of Nigeria. The meeting noted that these states witnessed mass killings from the herdsmen/farmer clashes. In order to also curtail the movements of herdsmen in the affected states, they are to make land available for ranches. Accordingly, the ranches would enable herdsmen and their families to be able to access good medical facilities and good schools for their children in the ranches. The ranching would also improve the well-being of the cattle. Similarly, the Federal Government of Nigeria proposed cattle colony as a solution to the reoccurring clashes between Fulani herdsmen and farmers. Though some states such as Plateau, Nasarawa and Kogi states have indicated interest of keying into Cattle Colony proposal, some groups in Kogi state cautioned the state Governor, Yahaya Bello, asking him to thread softly to avoid any looming disaster that will follow, such as open invitation of herdsmen. A group known as 'project Igala', consisting of people from Kogi East and cutting across nine local government areas namely Ankpa, Bassa, Dekina, Ibaji, Idah, Igalamela/Odulu, Ofu, Olamaboro and Omala local government areas has dissociated themselves from the purported plan to situate any cattle colony in their land (Daily Post, January 18, 2018). John Akinfehinwa of the Dailypost(2018) online, noted that the group in a petition written to President Muhammadu Buhari, pointed out that the move by Governor Yahaya Bello to establish Cattle Colony in the Eastern part of Kogi state is not acceptable to the Igala people. They opposed the move because according to them it will eventually lead to breakdown of law and order with killings and wanton destruction of property because the people who are farmers are not prepared to host Fulani herdsmen or cattle colony masters in their land. Again, the group further reinforced their opposition to the cattle colony proposal by stating the multiple acts of war and mayhem being unleashed daily on the innocent farmers and law-abiding citizens in their villages are between June 2015 and December 2017, Igala land has witnessed several incidences of killings as a result of herdsmen violence in areas including Ebeje where 8 people were killed and farms set ablaze, Agbada/Agojeju where 19 persons were killed, Edede where 2 persons were killed, in Oganenigu-6 persons killed, 3 persons killed in Ojapata, 5 persons were killed in Ojuwo Anawo. All in Dekina local government area of Kogi state. In Ofu local government area, Ojowu Omachi and Akpagidigbo where incessant attacks by herdsmen have claimed the lives of over 20 persons. In Abejukolo and Bagang villages of Omala local government area, the terror resonate loudly, so much so that the people no longer move freely to and from their farm lands because they fear being killed, maimed and rape. In some villages such as Ebakume, the entire village was sacked and their entire farm produce, granaries/silos completely burnt (John Akinfehinwa, 2018). The group further decried insecurity in the areas mentioned above and feared that despite the brazen nature of the aforementioned acts by the Fulani herdsmen who would be the occupants of the so-called cattle colony enjoyed subtle protection and favouritism, and none of them has been arrested or made to account for these crimes. They are heavily armed, terrorizing their land, flaunting their prowess in the handling of AK47 rifles and double barred guns. They have now treat Nigeria as a conquered territory where they go beyond destroying farmlands but move about maiming and killing at the slightest provocation. The group maintains that:

> We do not want cattle colony or grazing reserve in our land. We reject any attempt to convert or transfer the ownership of ancestral lands or transfer the ownership of ancestral lands in Igala land to cattle colony master or owners who operate by killing people, destroying communities wholesale, and destroying farmlands while enjoying government protection from counter attack, arrest or prosecution. We reject attempts to turn Igala land into the next killing field of marauding Fulani herdsmen" (Daily Post, 2018).

The proposed ranching and cattle colonies were rejected by Benue State government and went ahead to enact the anti grazing law, Osun state government rejected the ranching which was made public by the state's commissioner for information and strategy on January 18, 2018. However, the Osun state government had set up a committee comprising of government officials, farmers and herdsmen to resolve any issue which may result in conflict (Nurudeen, 2018). Ekiti state not only rejected it but also established its anti grazing law. Furthermore, movements of herdsmen from neighbouring West African countries would be required to show some travel documents. The Minister of Agriculture, Augu Ogbe who was part of the NEC meeting pointed out that ECOWAS protocol on free movement of persons may no longer be practiced in Nigeria (Naija.ng, 26th April, 2018). The Federal Government will no longer allow the killings to continue.

However, in Plateau state, a group under the aegis of concerned Run/Kulere people in Bokkos Local government area of Plateau state, called for the adoption of livestock alimentation practice as a panacea to the frequent herders/farmers clashes in the country (Daily Post, 19th April, 2018). Pwanagba (2018) citing briefing by Makut Macham to journalists in Jos where Macham was quoted to have said:

> After deep reflection and a review of experiences of herders and crop farmers, we have come to a conclusion that livestock alimentation practice is the safest

and most effective approach to resolving that attacks of herders on crop farmers in Nigeria… in simple terms, livestock alimentation practice involves a system of keeping animals within a confined space, and providing them with adequate nutritional and medical care without having to expose them to open grazing in the countryside for pasture."

The purposed alimentation practice seeks to replicate the existing practices in poultry farming for cows, pigs, goats, sheep among other (Pwanagba, Daily post, 2018). Further stressing on the practice, Macham also noted that it will require a transformation of the existing cattle paddocks, otherwise known as "hoggo" in Fulfulde or "Shinge" in Hausa, to feedlots. He also emphasized that the alimentation practice or feedlot system of cattle breeding was successfully employed to resolved Tutsi/Hutu genocide in Rwanda and is also successfully practice in Ethiopia (Pwanagba, Dailypost, 2018).

Again Pwanagba (2018) asserted that Macham stated the importance of the alimentation practice to the government, the herdsmen and farmers. According to him, the policy has a strong potential to rouse a symbiosis between livestock herders and crop farmers, as well as spur the emergence of a new economy at the grass root level. He maintained that: "In pursuing the livestock alimentation practice, government at every level would need to develop livestock-specific financing scheme and also provide subsidies as is done elsewhere in the world for agriculture. At the end of it all the policy will bring to end the rampant attacks of herders on farmers in Nigeria. The menace that characterized our socio-economic system and denied Nigerians the much needed zeal to flourish in their developmental strides.

Effects of Fulani Herdsmen and Farmers' Conflict on intergroup Relation and Corporate Existence of Nigeria

To demonstrate the effect of climate change and on the Fulani herders and farmers relationship in Nigeria, climate change increase atmospheric temperature depletion of the ozone layer and increase in ocean temperature. More ocean, sea and river floods are also being experienced as a result of warmer temperature which cause evaporation and lead to heavier rain falls in some regions of Nigeria. Climate change also cause rising sea level, ocean acidification, heat waves, and threat to biodiversity such as plant and animals population, rivers and lakes, protected covers and habitats. Land use activities that affect climate change include irrigation, deforestation, agricultural activities, road and building construction, dumping of solid waste and burning of wastes which are done without control by the authorities. They essentially affect and change the environment by changing the amount of water going into and out of a place; influence the ground cover and change the quantity of sunlight that is absorbed. Deforestation as a result of construction of either houses or roads and other infrastructure for developmental purposes can lead to desertification. More recently, temperatures in some cities have risen, with much higher increase in urban areas due to extensive human development of the landscape. These deforestation and land use activities denies the herders cattle food and water along their grazing routs. The issue of climate change which has devastating consequences for the herders in the far northern states, with its effect on rainfall affecting water reserves and fodders for animal feeds has led to shift south ward of the Sahara desert resulting in the desertification and soil degradation in some parts of Nigeria. This has resulted in the Fulani herdsmen increase movement south wards in search of food and water for themselves in the states of the North Central Nigeria. These movements often pitch the Fulani herdsmen in violent conflicts with the farmers. Herders also accuse natives along grazing routes of stealing their cows and this leads to clashes, thus affecting the cordial relationship between them.

Since the return of civil rule in Nigeria in 1999, farmers- herders' conflict and violence has contributed to loss of thousands of lives and destruction several properties worth millions or billions of Naira. It also displaced tens of thousands of people from their communities and villages. This created enemity and haterate for Fulani herdsmen by farmers and community members in the affected state of Benue, Nasarawa, Kogi and Niger. Infact, the situation is that the Fulani herdsmen are viewed as security risk and no longer welcome in some states and communities. For instance, in Kogi state the Igala people decried insecurity in their communities and feared that despite the brazen nature of the violent acts by the Fulani herdsmen who would be the occupants of the so-called cattle colony enjoyed subtle protection and favouritism, and none of them has been arrested or made to account for these crimes. They are heavily armed, terrorizing their land, flaunting their prowess in the handling of AK47 rifles and double barred guns. They have now treat Nigeria as a conquered territory where they go beyond destroying farmlands but move about maiming and killing at the slightest provocation. They reject attempts to turn Igala land into the next killing field of marauding Fulani herdsmen (Daily Post, 2018). In Benue State, Fulani and farmers relation has turned soar since the government went ahead to enact the anti grazing law. The Tiv and Fulani who are playmates according to legend no longer want to relate with each other. Farmers in the state which is tagged *the food basket of the nation*, are afraid to go to the farm with the raining season on. The crisis in the state has even taken a religious dimension after the killing of the Catholic Bishops and the 17 followers. Apart from climate change, since the founding of Nigeria's fourth republic in 1999, the country has been experiencing communal, ethnic, religious, political agitations. These leads to breakdown of law and order, insecurity and violence. Insecurity and insurgency by Boko Haram sect in the Northeast Nigeria have led many populations to create self-defense forces, ethnic militias, state run militias, armed gangs, vigilante groups which have been used to engage in further violence. In modern era, many Fulani abandoned their pastoralist, nomadic way of life in favour of sedentary way of life. They now engage in kidnappings, militias and cattle rustlers. The question is who will relate with the Fulani herdsmen and provide space for them. Even now most states in the federation are waring of them and treat them with disdain and caution.

Conclusion and Recommendations

Fulani herdsmen-farmers conflict has raged intensively in Nigeria especially in the North Central states. The use of sophisticated weapons by the Fulani against the civilians is generating anxiety among Nigerians and international communities. The intensity and nature of attacks on villages by the Fulani herdsmen in some states of the North Central Nigeria and other parts of the country have generated insinuations from analyst and opinion leaders that it may be handwork of political elements and government sponsored militias. Nairaland (2018) cited Kalu, a former Governor of Abia State stating that those killing Nigerians are not Fulani herdsmen. Also a research conducted by Chinua

Achebe Centre for Leadership and Dvelopment (CACLAD) reported by Adisa (2018) found that there is a group of Fulani herdsmen who rear the cattle from the north to the south, who could not speak English and are so poor as they are paid just a little amount of money for their job. They do not carry guns but only carry arrows machetes to help navigate the bushes. It concluded that when people talk about a herdsmen attack, it must be understood that the attacks are well coordinated and sometimes involves the approval of senators and influential men in Abuja. The fact is that climate change has its effect some parts of Nigeria resulting in the movement of these groups of people in search of pastures and water for their cattle. A hitherto simple nomads have suddenly become hostile to the communities they came across in the course of their migration. Even in States where there has been symbiotic relationship, the situation has degenerated into clashes and conflicts resulting in the destruction of lives and properties and strain relationships between the Fulani herdsmen and farmers, and communities and villages in the North Central states. The paper finds that climate change is a serious threat to the socio-economic activities of the Fulani herdsmen in Northern Nigeria. Furthermore, the Fulani herdsmen are forced to migrate to other states with favourable climatic conditions. They are viewed as threats and this lead to conflicts between the host communities and the Fulani herdsmen leading to loss of lives and properties and serious effect on intergroup relations.

The paper recommends the creation of large acres of ranches called the cattle colony across the country which should be allotted to the Fulani herdsmen, the colony is much larger and viable cheaper and safer because the colonies will have several ranches in them where the government should provide water and feeds at a subsidized rate. The government should sensitize and educate the host communities and the Fulani herdsmen on the need for ranching and peaceful co-habitation and national integration.

Government should explore other means of resolving the conflict since proposed measures such as Cattle colonies and ranches are heavily resisted and use of law enforcement to resolve conflict have proved deficient and counterproductive due to accusations leveled against the military and police of taking side with one group.

Government should hasting in yielding to the yearnings of the Fulani herdsmen by creating grazing routes in each state as well as mount vigorous enlightenment programme for the Fulani herdsmen and farmers as well as the general public on the need to embrace peaceful co-existence harmony and integration.

Implementation of the Paris Climate Agreement within the United Nation framework Convention on Climate Change (UNFCCC) should be taken seriously in order to achieve an increase in global average temperature to 1.5 C above pre-industrial levels.

It is recommended that Nigeria should join the membership of the Climate Vulnerable Forum (CVF); a 43 nation group of the most vulnerable countries that negotiate as a bloc at the UNFCCC which maintain the lethargy that showcase the way our leaders handle such issues of great importance.

Further recommendation is that the best ways and means to tackle climate change problems is to explore various opportunities they present to empower mostly people towards investing in power sector to cut down gas emission and exploring opportunities in wastewater recycling for irrigation in the northern part of Nigeria, and also to create jobs and stop a naturally-induced crisis from becoming politically explosive as being witnessed in the middle belt region of Nigeria.

References

Alao, D.O. (2015). Conflicts and Peace in Africa and Middle East. In D. Alao (ed). *Issues in Conflict, Peace & Governance.* Ibadan: Fodnab Ventures

Adesina, F. (2018). Why I Declared Intentions Now, by President Buhari. This Day Newspaper 11th, April, 2018.

Adisa, C. (2018). Research Findings of Chinua Achebe Centre for Leadership and Development. Nairaland Forum. Retrieved on 24th May, 2018 at 4.24 pm

Akinfehinwa, J. (2018). You Don't Own Kogi State- Community Leader warns Governor Bello Over Cattle Colony. Daily Post Online Retrieved on 25th April, 2018 at 14:35pm

Bilyaminu, S.M. (2015). Sustainable Environmental Development and Vulnerability to Climate Change Hazards in Nasarawa State, Nigeria. In B. Tijjani, M. Idris, N.M. Habib M.Y. Kurfi (eds). *Proceedings of 1st International Conference and Doctoral Colloquium.* Organized by Faculty of Social and Management Sciences, Bayero University, Kano, Nigeria. Nov.16-18.

Baker, S. (2006). Sustainable Development. Oxon: Routhedge

Burton, G. (2017). Background Report: The Fulani Herdsmen, Part1 Key Findings, Introduction, And History. The Project Cyma, online retrieved 25th May, 2018 at 5.20 pm

Daily Post (2018). Fulani Herdsmen and Farmers Clashes in Benue State. Dailypost,ng. Retrieved on 25th April, 2018 at 12. 00 pm

Dresner, S. (2002). *The Principles of Sustainability.* London: Earth Scan

Ewubare, K. (2018). FG Bans Movement of Herdsmen in Benue, Taraba States. www.naija.ng. Retrieved on 27 April, 2018 at 9.30 am

Godwin, C.A. (2018). Herdsmen Strike in Benue, Kill Reverend Fathers, 17 Others. Daily Post Online. Retrieved on 25th April, 2018 at 11.45 am

Godwin, C.A. (2018). Plateau Boils, Three Killed, Village Razed in Communal Clash. Daily Post Online. Retrieved on 25th April, 2018 at 12.10 pm

Godwin, C.A. (2018). Herdsmen Kill Four Construction Workers in Plateau. Daily Post Online. Retrieved on 25th April, 2018 at 12.35 pm

Ichoku, H.E (2005) Income redistributive effects of the healthcare financing system in Nigeria. Research Paper

Naija.ng (2018). History of Fulani Herdsmen in Nigeria and Today's Cisis. www.naija.ng

Nurudeen, L. (2018). 9 Important facts you should know about Herders-Farmers Conflict in Nigeria. Naij. Com. Retrieved on 23rd May, 2018, at 11.45am

Okolo, D.A. (2010). *Global Climate Change; Causes, Effects, Impact, Mitigation: A Theoretical And Practical Perspective.* Oweri: Alphabet Nigeria Publishers

Pwanagba, A. (2018). Plateau Killings: Another 8 Murdered at Relaxation Sport. Daily Post Online. Retrieved on 25th April, 2018 at 12.48 pm.

Pwanagba, A. (2018). Plateau Group Reveals what can End Herdsmen, Farmers Clashes. Daily Post Oline. Retrieved on 25th April, 2018 at 1.00 pm

Silas, D. (2018). Kogi Killings: Gunmen Attack on Community Spreads, Death toll now 17. Daily Post Online. Retrieved on 25th April, 2018 at 12.00 pm

Udo, U. & Adoyi, O. (2016). *Peace Studies and Conflict Resolution: Compilation of Notes.* Keffi: AMD Designs & Communication

UNHCR (2014). Country Operations Profile Africa. www.unhcr.org/pages/49e45 ade6. html. Retrieved on 3rd April, 2018.

Strategic Assessment of Dark Web and Cybercrime Threat Mitigation in Nigeria

BY

EBUTE, JOEL U., PhD, MCP, MCSA, MCDBA, MCSE, CCNA, CCNP, CEH, CFI, CSA,

ABSTRACT

The study was carried out to strategically assess dark web and cybercrime threat mitigation in Nigeria. The population of this study comprised all professionals in computer science, computer engineering and security agents who have been exposed to cybercrimes, cyber security and general computer science. The study adopted a descriptive survey design, while stratified random sampling technique was used in selecting 400 respondents. The instrument for data collection, which was tagged "Dark Web and Cybercrime Threat Mitigation Questionnaire (DWCTMQ) ", was administered to the respondents and used for the study. Data collected were analyzed using percentage analysis, mean statistics and goodness of fit chi-square analysis. From the results of the data analysis, it was observed that there is high level of dark web and cybercrimes activities in Nigeria. It was also observed that there are various types of threats caused by dark web and cybercrimes in Nigeria including stealing of data, havoc on individuals and organizations by the criminals, advanced persistent threats, distributed denial of service attacks, botnets, destructive malware, the growing challenge of ransom ware etc. One of the recommendations was that cyber security should be seen by all as a shared responsibility which requires the attention of a broad range of stakeholders with effective public/private partnership that incorporates businesses and institutions of all sizes to produce successful outcomes in identifying and addressing threats, vulnerabilities and overall risk in cyberspace.

KEYWORDS: Dark Web, Cyber Crimes Activities, Cyber Threats, Nigeria

Introduction

In recent times, our society has been increasingly relying on the internet and other information technology tools to engage in personal communication and conduct business activities among other several benefits. While these developments allow for enormous gain in productivity, efficiency and communication, they also create a loophole which may totally destroy an organisation. The term cybercrime can be used to describe any criminal activity which involves the computer or the internet network (Okeshola, 2013). This term is used for crimes such as fraud, theft, blackmail, forgery, and embezzlement, in which computers or networks are used.

According to Moore (2005), cybercrime, or computer oriented crime, is crime that involves a computer and a network, the computer may have been used in the commission of a crime, or it may be the target. Warren, Kruse, Jay and Heiser (2002) asserted that cybercrimes can be defined as: "Offences that are committed against individuals or groups of individuals with a criminal motive to intentionally harm the reputation of the victim or cause physical or mental harm, or loss, to the victim directly or indirectly, using modern telecommunication networks such as Internet (networks including but not limited to chat rooms, emails, notice boards and groups) and mobile phones (Bluetooth/SMS/MMS)".

The Dark Web is a term that refers specifically to a collection of websites that exist on an encrypted network and cannot be found by using traditional search engines or visited by using traditional browsers. Almost all sites on the so-called Dark Web hide their identity using the Tor encryption tool. A relatively known source for content that resides on the dark Web is found in the Tor network. The Tor network is an anonymous network that can only be accessed with a special Web browser, called the Tor browser (Tor, 2014). It has the ability to hide ones identity and activity and also spoof your location so it appears you're in a different country to where you're really located, making it much like using a VPN service.

Paganini (2012) asserted that each day, our Web actions leave footprints by depositing personal data on the Internet. This information composes our digital identity, our representation in cyberspace. Internet anonymity is guaranteed when Internet Protocol (IP) addresses cannot be tracked. Tor client software routes Internet traffic through a worldwide volunteer network of servers, hiding user's information and eluding any activities of monitoring. This makes the dark Web very appropriate for cybercriminals, who are constantly trying to hide their tracks (Paganini 2012). The dark Web is also the preferred channel for governments to exchange documents secretly, for journalists to bypass censorship of several states and for dissidents to avoid the control of authoritarian regimes (Gehl, 2014). Anon)

Communications have an important place in our political and social discourse. Many individuals wish to hide their identities due to concerns about political or economic retribution. The dark web also hosts markets of illegal goods (such as counterfeit products, drugs, and IDs) and financial crime services (such as money laundering and bank frauds). It hosts markets offering paedophilia content, hitman services, conventional and chemical weapons purchase, and illegal medical research.

According to Maitanmi (2013), responding to cybercrime is even more challenging because the economics favor the criminals. With just a laptop, a single individual can wreak havoc on individuals and organizations with minimal cost and little risk of being caught. More advanced technologies and protective measures will eventually deter nefarious conduct, help security officers catch and prosecute perpetrators and level what has become an unbalanced playing field. This study therefore seeks to strategically assess dark web and cybercrime threat mitigation in Nigeria.

Over the years, the alarming growth of the internet and its wide acceptance has led to increase in security threats, In Nigeria today, several internet assisted crimes known as cybercrimes are committed daily in various forms such as fraudulent electronic mails, pornography, identity theft, hacking, cyber harassment, spamming, Automated Teller Machine spoofing, piracy and phishing. Cybercrime and crimes committed in the dark web are threat against various institutions and people who are connected to the internet either through their computers or mobile technologies. The exponential increase of this crime in the society has become a strong issue that should not be overlooked. The impact of this kind of crime can be felt on the lives, economy and international reputation of a nation. Lack of strong cybercrime laws has encouraged the perpetrators to commit more crime knowing that they can always go uncaught. There is the need for our government to come up with policies that address cybercrime and the nefarious activities done on the dark web and enforce such laws so that criminals will not go unpunished. This study therefore seeks to strategically assess dark web and cybercrime threat mitigation in Nigeria.

The main objective of the study is to strategically assess dark web and cybercrime threats mitigation in Nigeria, while the specific objectives are as follows: To examine the level of dark web and cybercrimes activities in Nigeria. And To find out the types of threats caused by dark web and cybercrimes in Nigeria.

The following research questions will be addressed: What is the level of dark web and cybercrimes activities in Nigeria? And What are the types of threats caused by dark web and cybercrimes in Nigeria? The null hypotheses to be tested is; there is no significant difference in the perception of people as regards the level of dark web and cybercrimes activities in Nigeria.

LITERATURE REVIEW

Level of Dark Web and Cyber Crimes Activities in Nigeria

Cybercrime and dark web activities are trends that are gradually growing as the internet continues to penetrate every sector of our society and no one can predict its future. The crime usually requires a hectic task to trace. Sui, Caverlee and Rudesill (2015) asserted that when it comes to the availability of fake goods, everything from counterfeit train tickets to drugs and passports can be found on the dark web. While some consumers purposely seek out places to purchase items on the Deep Web, many internet users find these sites inadvertently or are purposely directed there through suspect links on social media platforms or websites.

Colbaugh and Glass (2012) opined that vast quantities of private information, such as log-in credentials, banking and credit card details, are peddled with impunity on crypto-marketplaces. Cybercriminals also offer their services for hire and even provide tutorials on code-breaking and how to infiltrate corporate networks. Cybercrime itself has become a service that is offered pervasively on the Dark Web. With Bitcoin used as the preferred currency, every transaction between buyer and seller can be conducted anonymously on the Dark Web.

According to Abbasi and Chen (2010), most of the content on the Deep Web contains information for legitimate uses -including corporate intranets or academic resources residing behind a firewall, social media sites hidden behind a log-in page, online forms, pop-up ads and pages that are unlinked to other sites. However, some sites on the Deep Web also represent potentially unauthorised or suspicious content, such as phishing sites that collect user credentials, sites that disseminate mal ware, websites and marketplaces that sell counterfeit goods and peer-to-peer sites where piracy often takes place. Consumers may unknowingly stumble upon these unauthorised sites through spam emails, advertisements or cyber squatted domains, and are at risk of unwittingly releasing personal information or credentials to fraudulent entities (Abbasi and Chen, 2010).

French, Epiphaniou and Maple (2013) asserted that deeper beneath the surface layer of the Internet lies the Dark Web, a smaller but potentially more dangerous subset of the Deep Web. The Dark Web is the collection of websites and content that exists on dark nets – overlay networks whose Internet Protocol addresses are completely hidden. Both publishers and visitors to Dark Web sites are entirely anonymous. Dark Web content can be accessed only by using special software such as Tor, Freenet, Invisible Internet Project and Tails. Tor is free to download and use, and enables anonymous access and communication within the Dark Net. Around 2.5 million people access Dark Web content through Tor daily. It is often used by strong privacy advocates, such as journalists and law enforcement agencies that may be searching for dangerous or sensitive information and do not want their online activity tracked. The very anonymity of the Dark Web makes it an ideal foundation for illicit activity.

According to Lakshmi (2015), as at 2003, the United States and South-Korea highest cyber-attacks of 35.4% and 12.8% respectively. With the population of Nigeria placed at 160 million from the last census carried out in 2006, a recent statistics revealed that about 28.9% have access to the internet (Hassan, 2012). It was also proven that 39.6% African users of internet are actually Nigerians, hence, the high increase in the rate of internet crime in Nigeria (Hassan, 2012). Presently, cybercrimes are performed by people of all ages ranging from young to old, but in most instances the young.

In Nigeria, cybercrime has become one of the main avenues for pilfering money and business espionage. According to Check Point, a global network cyber security vendor, as of 2016, Nigeria was ranked 16th highest country in cyber-attacks vulnerabilities in Africa (Ewepu, 2016). Nigerians are known both home and abroad to be rampant perpetuators of cybercrimes. The number of Nigerian caught for duplicitous activities carried by broadcasting stations are much more in comparison to other citizens of different countries. The contribution of the internet to the development of Nigeria has had a positive impact on various sectors of the country. However, these sectors such as the banking, e-commerce and educational sector battles with the effect of cybercrimes. More cybercrimes are arising at an alarming rate with each subsequent crime more advanced than its predecessor.

Generally, cybercrime may be divided into one of two types of categories: Crimes that affects computer networks and devices directly. Examples are malicious code, computing viruses, mal-ware etc. Crimes facilitated by computer networks or devices, the primary target of which is independent of the computer networks or device. Examples include Cyber Stalking, Fraud and identity theft, phishing scams and information warfare.

Types of Threats Caused by Dark Web and Cyber Crimes in Nigeria

Cyber threat can be defined as criminal activities involving an IT infrastructure. Cyber threats in Nigeria started late 1990s, and have continued to escalate in variation and frequency. Efforts to fight cyber threats have involved a growing number of participants including governments, non-governments, public sectors, and non-profit organizations. According to Akinsuyi (2009), threats are categorized into four different forms: attack through email, spam associated threats, mal ware and phishing. Malware threat was further described to reduce system network. Hence, on the case of threats to email, this disallows employees to have access to the original data of the organization. Phishing threats on the other hand, are in form of hacking of vital information, especially hacking of credit card information or account information. The common types of threats caused by dark web and cybercrimes in Nigeria include:

Phishing: Phishing is simply the theft of an identity. It involves stealing personal information from unsuspecting users and it is also an act of fraud against the authentic, authorised businesses and financial institutions that are victimized (Wada and Odulaja, 2014). Phishing scams are ubiquitous and are exponentially increasing. It has become one of the fastest growing cybercrimes in Nigeria. Fraudsters have devised a means to mimic authorised organisations and retrieve confidential information from clients. In Phishing email messages, the fraudsters find a way to convince and gain the trust of users. In Nigeria, phishing mails are mostly carried out on bank customers.

Cyber-theft/Banking Fraud: Hackers target the vulnerabilities in the security of various bank systems and transfer money from innumerable accounts to theirs. Most cyber-criminals transfer bantam amounts like 5 naira which are sometimes overlooked by the user without questions raised by the users who assumes this was deducted for either SMS or ATM withdrawal charges. Doing this for over a million accounts enriches most fraudsters (Parthiban and Raghavan, 2014).

Cyber-Pornography: Cyber-pornography is the act of using cyberspace to create, display, distribute, import, or publish pornography or obscene materials, especially materials depicting children engaged in sexual acts with adults. Cyber-pornography is a criminal offense, classified as causing harm to persons.

Hacking: This is a type of crime wherein a person's computer is broken into so that his personal or sensitive information can be accessed. In hacking, the criminal uses a variety of software to enter a person's computer and the person may not be aware that his computer is being accessed from a remote location (Denning, 1999). In the United States, hacking is classified as a felony and punishable as such. This is different from ethical hacking, which many organizations use to check their Internet security protection.

Yahoo Attack: Also called 419, it is characterized by using e-mail addresses obtained from the Internet access points, using e-mail address harvesting applications (web spiders or e-mail extractor).

These tools can automatically retrieve e-mail addresses from web pages and send messages to unsuspecting victims defrauding them of their cash.

Credit Card or ATM Fraud: Credit card or ATM numbers can be stolen by hackers when users type the credit card number into the Internet page of the seller for online transaction or when withdrawing money using A TM card. The hackers can abuse this card by impersonating the credit card holder.

Ransomware: This is one of the detestable malware-based attacks. Ransomware enters your computer network and encrypts your files using public-key encryption, and unlike other malware this encryption key remains on the hacker's server. Attacked users are then asked to pay huge ransoms to receive this private key (Choo, 2007).

DDoS attacks: DDoS attacks are used to make an online service unavailable and bring it down, by bombarding or overwhelming it with traffic from multiple locations and sources. Large networks of infected computers, called Botnets are developed by planting malware on the victim computers. The idea is normally to draw attention to the DDOS attack, and allow the hacker to hack into a system. Extortion and blackmail could be the other motivations (Barford and Yegneswaran, 2007).

METHODS

Research Design

A descriptive survey design was used for this study. This was for the purpose of describing the extent and the effect of dark web and cybercrime threats and the extent of mitigation of these treats in Nigeria. The population of this study comprised all professionals in computer science, computer engineering and security agents who have been exposed to cybercrimes, cyber security and general computer science. A stratified random sampling technique was used to draw the 400 respondents and used for the study. The main instrument used in this study was questionnaire titled *"Dark Web and Cybercrime Threat Mitigation Questionnaire (DWCTMQ)"*. The obtained data was coded statistically before the statistical analysis of the data.

RESULTS AND DISCUSSIONS

Research Question One

What is the level of dark web and cybercrimes activities in Nigeria? Table I was used to answer the research question.

Table 1:
Percentage analysis of the level of dark web and cybercrimes activities in Nigeria

Level of dark web and cybercrime activities	Freq	%	Remarks
Very High	241	60.25**	1**
High	123	30.75	2nd
Low	25	6.25	3rd
Very Low	11	2.75*	4th*
TOTAL	**400**	**100%**	

** The highest percentage frequency
* The least percentage frequency
Source: Field Survey

The result in Table 1 shows the level of dark web and cybercrimes activities in Nigeria. From the result, it was observed that 60.25% of the respondents affirmed very high level of dark web and cybercrimes activities in Nigeria. 30.75% of the respondents affirmed high level, 6.25% of the respondents affirmed low level and 2.75% of the respondents affirmed very low level of dark web and cybercrimes activities in Nigeria. The result therefore means that there is high level of dark web and cybercrimes activities in Nigeria.

Research Question Two

What are the types of threats caused by dark web and cybercrimes in Nigeria? Table 2 was used to answer the research question.

Table 2:
Percentage analysis of the types of threats caused by dark web and cybercrimes in Nigeria

Dark web and cybercrimes threats	Freq	%	Remarks
Stealing of data	33	8.25	6th
Havoc on individuals and organizations by the criminals	45	11.25	5th
Advanced persistent threats	59	14.75	4th
Distributed denial of service attacks	26	6.5	7th
Botnets	62	15.5	3rd
Destructive malware	71	17.75	2nd
The growing challenge of ransom ware	104	26	1st
TOTAL	**400**	**100%**	

** The highest percentage frequency
* The least percentage frequency

From the result of the above table 2, it was observed that the highest types of threats caused by dark web and cybercrimes in Nigeria was "The growing challenge of ransom ware" 104 (26%) while the least one was "Distributed denial of service attacks" 6.5(6.5%).

Hypotheses Testing

Hypothesis One

The null hypothesis states that there is no significant difference in the perception of people as regards the level of dark web and cybercrimes activities in Nigeria. To test the hypothesis, chi-Square analysis was performed on the data (see table 3).

Table 3:
Chi-square analysis of the difference in the perception of people as regards the level of dark web and cybercrimes activities in Nigeria

Level of Dark Web and Cyber Crimes activities	Observed Freq	Expected Freq	X^2
VERY HIGH	241	100	
HIGH	123	100	
LOW	25	100	
VERY LOW	11	100	
TOTAL	**400**	**400**	

***Significant at 0.05 level; df= 3; Critical = 7.82**

Table 3 shows the calculated X^2-value as (339.56). This value was tested for significance by comparing it with the critical X^2-value (7.82) at 0.05 levels with 3 degree of freedom. The calculated X^2-value (339.56) was greater than the critical X^2-value (7.82). Hence, the result was significant. The result therefore means that there is significant difference in the perception of people as regards the level of dark web and cybercrimes activities in Nigeria. The significance of the result caused the null hypothesis to be rejected while the alternative one was accepted.

Discussion of the Findings

The result of the data analysis in table 3 was significant due to the fact that the calculated X^2-value (339.56) was greater than the critical X^2-value (7.82) at 0.05 level with 3 degree of freedom. The result implies that there is significant difference in the perception of people as regards the level of dark web and cybercrimes activities in Nigeria. The result therefore was in agreement with the research findings of Akinsuyi (2009) who highlighted that threats are categorized into four different forms: attack through email, spam associated threats, malware and phishing. Malware threat was further described to reduce system network. The significance of the result caused the null hypotheses to be rejected while the alternative one was accepted.

Conclusions and Recommendations

Based on the findings of the research work, it was concluded that there are many cases of dark web and cybercrimes activities in Nigeria. There is high level of dark web and cybercrimes activities in Nigeria. There is significant difference in the perception of people as regards the level of dark web and cybercrimes activities in. Nigeria.

The following recommendations are deemed necessary:

1. Cyber security should be seen by all as a shared responsibility which requires the attention of a broad range of stakeholders with effective public/private partnership that incorporates businesses and institutions of all sizes along with national, state, local, tribal and territorial agencies to produce successful outcomes in identifying and addressing threats, vulnerabilities and overall risk in cyberspace.
2. Individual consumers in Nigeria should also have a role of crying out the task of propagating incidence and threats of dark web to the general public for precaution.
3. Education should be rendered to people on how to better protect themselves from the threat of dark web and cybercrimes in Nigeria.

References

Abbasi, A. & Chen, D. (2010) *The Manager's Handbook for Corporate Security*: Establishing and Managing a Successful Assets Protection Program. Butterworth-Heinemann, USA.

Choo, K. R. (2007) "The Cyber Threat Landscape: Challenges and Future Research Directions." *Computers & Security* 30, no. 8 (November 2011): 719-31. doi: 10.10 16(j .cose.20 11.08.004.

Denning, D. E. (1999). *Information Warfare and Security*, ACM Press, USA.

Ewepu, G. (2016). *Nigeria loses N127bn annually to cyber-crime* - NSA available at: http://www.vanguardngr.com/2016/04/nigeria-loses-n127bn-annually- cybercrime -nsa/Retrieved Jun. 9, 2016.

French, c., Epiphaniou, M. & Maple, H. (2013)Retrieved September 10, 2011 from http//www.guide2nigeria.com/news_articles_AboutNig

Gehl, R. W. (2014). *"Power/Freedom on the Dark Web: A Digital Ethnography of the DarkWeb Social Network."* New Media & Society, October

http *Fighting Cyber Crime in Nigeria.*://nms.sagepub.com/content/early/20 14/1 011611461444 814554900.full#ref-38.

Hassan, A. B. (2012) Cybercrime in Nigeria: Causes, Effects and the Way Out, ARPN *Journal of Science and Technology*, vol. VOL. 2(7),626 - 631.

Lakshmi, P. M. (2015), Cyber Crime: Prevention & Detection," *International Journal of Advanced Research in Computer and Communication Engineering*, vol. Vol. 4(3).

Maitanmi, O. S. (2013), Impact of Cyber Crimes on Nigerian Economy, *The International Journal of Engineering and Science (IJES)*, Vol. 2 (4), 45-51.

Moore; B. (2005) International Communication Principles, Concepts and Issues. In Okunna,C.S. (ed) Techniques of Mass Communication: A Multi-dimentional Approach. Enugu: New

Generation Books. *Warren G. Kruse, Jay G. Heiser (2002). Computer forensics: incident response essentials. Addison-Wesley. p. 392. ISBN 0-201-70719-5.*

Okeshola, F. B. (2013) The Nature, Causes and Consequences of Cyber Crime in Tertiary Institutions in Zaria-Kaduna State, *Nigeria American International Journal of Contemporary Research*, vol. 3(9), 98-114.

Paganini, P. (2012). *The Good and the Bad of the Deep Web.* Security Affairs, September 17.

Parthiban, L. & Raghavan, A. R. (2014), The effect of cybercrime on a Bank's finances, *International Journal of Current Research and Academic Review,* Volume-2(2), no. ISSN: 2347-3215,173-178, Retrieved Feb. 2014 from www.ijcrar.com

Sui, D. J., Caverlee, D. & Rudesill, X. (2015). *"The Deep Web and the Dark Net."* Accessed August 30, 2016. https://www.wilsoncenter.org/publication/the-deep-web-and-the-darknet.

Tor. (2014)a. *Tor: Overview.* www.torproject.org/about/overview.html.en.

Tor. (20 14)b. *Inception.* www.torproject.org/about/torusers.html.en.

Wada, F. & Odulaja, G. O. (2014), Electronic Banking and Cyber Crime Tn Nigeria - A Theoretical Policy Perspective on Causation, *Afr J Comp & ICT*, Vol 4(3), no. Issue 2.

Peace and Security: Usage of Religion to Create Conflicts in African and its Peace-building Strategies.

BY

REV. LONGKAT DANIEL DAJWAN LECTURER GINDIRI
THEOLOGICAL SEMINARY, PLATEAU STATE NIGERIA
Email: longkadan@gmail.com Tel: 234 706 8134 337

FOCUS SCRIPTURES
*"WHEN A MAN'S WAYS ARE PLEASING TO THE LORD, HE MAKES
EVEN HIS ENEMIES LIVE AT PEACE WITH HIM (PROVERBS 16:7)"
AGAIN "IF IT IS POSSIBLE, AS FAR AS IT DEPENDS ON YOU, LIVE
AT PEACE EVERYONE (ROMANS 12:18 CF ROM.14:1-3; 13-19)"*

ABSTRACT

This article submits that religion has a dual legacy of peace and violence in Africa. It x-rays how the three religions in the continent (Islam, Christianity and African Traditional Religion) have been central to selected cases of frictions and how resources from the religions could be harnessed in the search for peace (structural conflict and structural peace). In doing this, the discussion alluded to the conversion of most Africans from their indigenous religion to the Abrahamic religions (Islam and Christianity) from the Arab expansion in the 8th century and European expansion in the 15th century. The article noted that the importation of these religions to Africa and the petition of the continent into entities for administrative convenience by Europeans in the twilight of the 19th century multiplied the primordial factors (cultural, historic, religious and identity differences) responsible for many conflicts in Africa. Other theories responsible for religious frictions in the continent were equally given significance. These theories include fundamentalism and instrumentalism. Fundamentalism speaks of extreme believe that create boundary lines among adherents of different faiths; while instrumentalism speaks of how greedy people use religion as a means for divide and rule. Several examples of conflicts with religious connotations were drawn from countries across Africa such as Nigeria, Sudan, Mali, Chad and Kenya. The narratives from the conflicts or frictions indicated that a single theory cannot sufficiently explain the reason for any of the conflicts. In analyzing Africa Traditional Religion (ATR), the article hazards the theory that adherents of indigenous faith align with their interest during conflicts between the Abrahamic faiths. Also, Moslems and some Christians are known to solicit protection power from ATR practitioners which gives them some form of energy and confidence. Such often fuels and sustains conflict in the continent. The article also recognizes religion as the search for the values of the ideal life and the personification of human ideals. It recommends the religious Market Place Theory and functionalist's theory as panaceas for religious tolerance and peace with it attendant true practice of godly values;

and maintains that values embedded in the three faiths should be harnessed as strategic guides against corruption and social injustice which are key impediments to economic development and peace of the society and the church. Tools in ATR such as Gacaca and Ubuntu where also recommended as strategic guides in the search for peace.

1. INTRODUCTION:

Conflict and peace are dynamic concepts because they involve human relationship. It is unclear whether religions can be said to be a cause of conflict or peace in any given pluralistic society. Similarly, it is easy to assume that all religions profess peace and should be accepted as having nothing to do with conflict. However, there is a truism that violent conflicts have been associated with religion throughout the ages (Best 2011). Indeed, religion has a dual legacy of peace and violence from time immemorial to contemporary times (Gopin, 1997). The issue of conflict, with its sometimes attendant violence, has created both challenges to, and opportunities for peace and security to mankind since creation.

- The story of Cain and Abel in the Bible (Genesis 4:1-16)
- Ancient empires and kingdoms have either survived or crumbled as a result of conflicts
- 30 Years war in Europe- 23 May 1618-15 May 1648
- The Napoleonic Wars- 18 May 1803-20 November 1815
- The First World War (WWI)-July 28, 1914-November 11, 1918
- The Second World War (WWI)-September 1, 1939-September 2 1945.
- Anti-colonial Wars-Wars of liberation-Mainly in Africa (Southern Africa)-one of which is 14th April, 1977.
- The Balkan Wars-Former Yugoslavia (Post-Cold War Wars-"New Wars")-one of which is of 1991-2002.
- Somalia, Leberia, Sierraleon, DR Congo, Nigeria
- The Arab Spring- Tunisia, Egypt, Libya, Syria etc. (Obadiah: 2016).

When you read the Bible from cover to cover, you will notice that there is much writing on the subject of conflict. Numerous examples of conflict are woven into the many stories of people's lives outlined in the scriptures. There is also much wisdom to be gleaned from the Bible on managing conflict. The Book of Proverbs is filled with a wealth insight on the causes of conflict, dealing with anger, and ending our disagreements with each other. The Bible gives us practical knowledge on the subject of conflict; Pastors and church leaders resist discussing church conflict, (nevertheless CONFLICT IS INEVITABLE BUT VIOLENCE IS AVOIDABLE). Their resistance often stems from the belief that all conflict is negative and to be avoided, if not ignored, at all costs. Someone said that conflict is either good or neither evil-only inevitable. The Bible seems to agree. Jesus made it clear that we would experience conflict even as Christians (Luke 17:1). Scripture lays out the proper way to handle conflict, and the Holy Spirit empowers us to deal with conflict competently, yet the church often remains unwilling to learn how to manage its conflicts in a way that will be beneficial to the kingdom of God (what a pity the friction going on in Assemblies of God Church). Conflict should be viewed as an opportunity to help people grow in faith. Rather than dwelling on the negative aspects of conflict in the church — divisiveness, power plays, and control issues (1Cor.3:1-23; 6:1-12) — the church should begin to recognize conflict as the ability and opportunity to create action from inaction. Conflict is so inevitable for Christians that Paul tells Timothy that all who desire to live godly lives in Christ Jesus will be persecuted (2 Timothy 3:12). Many Christians regard being in conflict as being in sin. It is not seen as a normal part of the Christian life. Yet Jesus has taught us, at some length, how to manage conflict and Proverbs has whole sections on it. **Conflict is inevitable for three reasons:**

   a.   Our knowledge is incomplete and imperfect so even sinless people in a perfect world will see the same situation differently through their own knowledge and perspectives.
   b.   Satan engineers conflict whenever and wherever possible especially amongst Christians. Satan sets us in conflict with ourselves, God and one another. (e.g Abraham and Lot's herdsmen in Genesis 13:1-8).
   c.   We knowingly enter into and initiate conflict with evil whenever we proclaim the gospel, preach holiness, protest against sin in our society, teach against cults or testify to Christ in the midst of a world and congregation that does not want to change.

Thus conflict is here to stay and we must learn to manage it in a Christian "Kingdom way" until Christ returns to take us home to heaven where there will be no more crying or sickness or pain.

We are made to believe that true Christians will never have conflict; this is not true as we saw in the scriptures above. Therefore, this course will undertake the following Fundamentals of Conflict management and Peace studies. It will highlight the definitions, description, basic understanding of Conflict management and Peace studies. The course will also explore the nature, types and stages of Conflict etc. With emphasis on approaches that are relevant to biblical Peace and the role of the Church in teaching Peace to the glory of God.

Indeed conflict and peace is a global reality. Africa has in no way been isolated as listed above from this debacle. Since Arab expansion in the eight century and European expansion in the fifteenth century, Africans have almost completely converted from their indigenous, traditional religions to Christianity and Islam. Has the transformation been for better or for worse? Nowhere does the relationship between religion and conflict become more tensed, dubious, controversial and suspicious than is the case between the Abrahamic religions, Christianity and Islam (Best, 2011). Although conflicts are caused by a number of factors, such as ethnicity and race, competition and resource distribution among others, religion has also been an integral component of some conflicts in Africa (cited in Dajwan 2018).

In the aspect of the natures of African conflicts are Group structure cannot be said to be static in any given society as there is always a continuous interaction among the individuals and groups that make up the society. One ground tends to dominate the other probably due to the constantly changing pattern of vested and competing interest. Under such a situation groups in such societies tend to protect their values for survival and advancement of their aspirations. Everyone thus has vested interest in the continuity and prosperity of his/her family or community. A society that is made up of such dominant group tendencies was bound to possess Keen competition, rivalry and conflict with regard to their values. This is because the interest of one groups are most often inconsistent with that of another. A political system that is dominated by these egocentric competitive tendencies often finds its segment or groups at logger heads and so can hardly survive the test of time. The problems of peaceful co-existence which pervaded the life of the Igbo during the pre-colonial period were the result of multiplicity of political, social and economic factors which included land ownership, kingship, territorial boundaries, murder and inheritance among others. Land epitomizes the socio-political and economic well-being of the individuals and communities. Walter Brueggemann (1978) posits that land is normally a place with historical meaning and provides continuity and identify across generations "where important words have been spoken, which have established identity, defined vocation and envisioned destiny..."

Religious conflicts are ideology based. They involve conflicts over identity, beliefs and values. The concept or term "value" is exposed in different life situations as significant in fulfilling our mental, emotional, spiritual or practical requirement. It may also simply be described as that which we find good or meaningful. It is very common to comment on the value of things that one prefers or likes and for which one may make conscious effort to acquire. But as human beings we are particularly struck by the values which we discerned in human relationships or in men's actions and behavior. Therefore, 'value' is a concept which is widely applied in man's life. In view of the variety and diversity of human life, the concept cannot be easily explained (Paul Roubickez). Values are precepts, beliefs, moral and spiritual principles and standard criteria of behavior/conduct which determine how people of a society, nation or state think and relate with one another. Examples are honesty, contentment, faithfulness, justices, tolerance, integrity, hard work, perseverance, and so on. The most important to remember is that "values are priceless, while valuables are priced" (E.g. of priced valuables are clothes, laptops and computers, houses, lands etc). In today's fast paced competitive world, man seems to have compromised on his values, integrity and character, in a bid to earn, use and possess more and more of material wealth, as a result, we see rampant corruption, unlawful activities, inhuman behavior and immoral consumption, which is slowly breaking the very structure of our society, nation and the world. Values are what a person what a person or group of persons consider worth doing in order to make life worth living and pleasant. It is a standard or quality of way of living considered to be worthwhile by a person or a group of persons by which he or they judge what is good and worth doing. As Roy Ponsner puts it, according to Pandang Yamsat (2012), "A value is a belief, a mission or a philosophy that is meaningful" to a person or a people. Thus, what we take as of value to us as individuals or as a group affects our work, attitude, our relational attitude to others, those in leadership positions or those not in leadership positions. So, values affect the way we work and the way we relate or behave towards other people, those who love us and those who do not love us. According to Imran (2013), the differences between values can be sources of conflict and conflict involving values are the most difficult to solve. Conflicts that are normally branded religious have deeper historical, cultural, social, political and economic under tones. (**Function of religion needed here**) The functions or benefits of religion to an individual of society includes all the human needs being socially, physically, economically, psychologically and spiritually.

Indeed, the article is to examine how religion has been used to create conflict in Africa and how the potentials of religion opportunities could be harnessed to enhance peaceful coexistence in the 21st pluralistic society. This presentation will focus on the three major religions in the continent: Christianity, Islam and African Traditional Religion. I will explain the manner through which the three religions have been used to create violence. Later at the course of the discussion will draw inspiration from how resources within the religions can be harnessed to manage conflicts.

02. CONCEPTUAL CLARIFICATION OF TERMS:

In search of a conceptual understanding the following concepts will be clarify as; religion, conflict, conflict management, peace, peace and security, peace building and pluralistic society;

a. RELIGION:

Like most religions, Christianity, Islam and African traditional religion are sets of believes, practices and perceptions centered on the divine. The Religious and Development Programme of the University of Birmingham understands religion as "set of beliefs concerning the supernatural, sacred or divine, and the moral codes, practices, values, institutions and rituals associated with such belief" (cited in Best, 2011:22). Religions have been generally conceptualized by scholars within substantive and functional frameworks. The substantive says what the religion is, and the functional says what the religion does (Gamaliel, 2011).

> *Spiro's substantive definition states that: Religion is: "An institution constituting of culturally patterned interaction with culturally postulated super beings". Greezt's functional definition on the other hand states that: Religion is a system of symbols which act to establish powerful, long lasting motivations in men…the motivations seem uniquely realistic (cited in Gamaliel, 2011:110).*

Religion cannot be defined by simple statements. Hayward in Best (2012) defines religion "as instructional framework within which specific theological doctrines and practices are advocated and pursued, usually among a community of likeminded believers". This includes the socio-political and economic structures that support such beliefs on one hand, and those that are continually produced in ideology, philosophy and social relationships. Religion is not easy to define although it is something man claims to know and practice throughout his lifespan. Some scholars defined religion as belief in one or more gods, or in supernatural beings. But this could not include all religions, because some religions may mean a way of living rather than a way of belief. According to world Encyclopedia-Britannica, Religion could best be defined as man's attempt to achieve the highest and possible good by adjusting his life to the strongest and best power in the universe. This power is usually called God. **"Religion is belief in someone else's experience. Spirituality is having your own experience."**– Deepak Chopra

Jones G. Vos (1975) gave the following definitions to religion:

1. Religion is the search for the values of the ideal life.
2. Religion is the recognition on the part of man of a controlling super human power entitled to obedience, reverence and worship.
3. Religion is a fact of human consciousness.
4. Religion is a man's response to what he believes to be the ultimate meaning of life.

5. True religion would have to be defined as man's proper response to the revelation of the true God. Still on what is religion? David, A. Brown (1990) gave another catalogue of definitions of religion as:
6. Religion is the beliefs of the community about God's relationship with the world.
7. Religion is the way in which the people of the community worship God and pray to him (cited Dajwan 2018).

It is equally important to highlight the views of scholars who see religion from a negative standpoint. First we begin with the popular view of Karl Max of religion as the opium of the masses. Lenin believes that the severe exploitation of the masses because of capitalism has caused poverty and forced the masses to turn to religion to "escape the life drudgery". According to Talcott Parson, religion is nothing but a palliative, a sort pf balm against frustration (Gamaliel, 2011).

Some fundamental concepts can be deduced in the conceptual understanding of religion which was painted above

- Religion may lead to the erection of cultural boundaries.
- Religion is a powerful motivation factor for adherents.
- Religion is uniquely realistic which explains why the vocal proponents preach their religions with a certain air of superiority.
- However, religion speaks of the highest human search of ideals value of life.

This speaks of the dual legacy of peace and violence of religion which I have earlier alluded to.

b. CONFLICT:

The friction arising from actual or perceived differences or incompatibilities

- Conflict is neutral- could be dangerous (dysfunctional) or it could also present opportunities (functional): the outcome depends on our attitude/responses (Dinshak: 2016).
- Paul says, "I hear that when you come together as a church, there are divisions among you, and to some extent I believe it" (1Cor. 11:18).
- The word "Conflict" comes from the Latin word con-fligere, meaning literally "to strike together". Whenever two or more people pursue mutually exclusive goals, or whenever one person's needs collide with another's conflict results. If there were no effort among humans to fulfill ideas, goals, or desires, there would be no conflict which is not possible.
- In their book Church Fights, Speed Leas and Paul Kittlaus helpfully distinguish three ways of in which conflict is experienced:
  i. **Intrapersonal Conflict**: the contest one has when different parts of the self-compete with one another. I want to beloved Pastor, but I also want to be preacher who speaks the truth.

ii. **Interpersonal Conflict:** personality differences that are not related primarily to issues. I like to think of myself as strong, independent person, but my administrative board chairperson treats me like an incompetent who must be told what to do.

iii. **Substantive Conflict:** disputes over facts, values, goals and beliefs (pluralistic society). I think we ought to put a new roof on the church, but the social concerns committee wants to open a clothes closet for the poor.

Again Obadiah Samuel gave the following definitions; what you possibly know about conflict:

- Fighting
- Disagreement
- Absence of peace
- Injustice
- Violence
- Clash
- Crisis
- War etc

The term 'Conflict' comes from the Latin word conflictus, which means collision or clash. There is no universally accepted definition of conflict. Defining conflict also depends on the concept one has of the nature of conflict as something that takes place in society and between people. For example, conflict is commonly understood as:

- a form of opposition between parties;
- an absence of agreement between parties;
- a way to solve social contradictions;
- a natural process in human social interaction.

Some scholarly definition:

c. CONFLICT MANAGEMENT:

- Conflict management is the principle that all conflicts cannot necessarily be resolved, but learning how to manage conflicts can decrease the odds of nonproductive escalation.
- Conflict management involves acquiring skills related to conflict resolution, self-awareness about conflict modes, conflict communication skills, and establishing a structure for management of conflict in a setting
- According to Dashan (2004) that the generic concept of conflict management is used interchangeably with the terms 'conflict control,' 'conflict regulation' and 'conflict resolution'. That Conflict management as a whole range of techniques employed in any society to prevent the development and escalation of conflict situations or once these have

developed, to prevent their resulting in disruptive and widely destructive conflict behavior through some form of settlement agreements.

- Management starts where prevention does not happen, when the conflict has started or had been and the step to manage it is pursued. Conflict management comes after the crisis has occurred. The role of the church is to be peace maker in a world full of wars and fights. The church is the only hope of peace in a war torn world (any learning/research/school that will not lead us to becoming solutions is not learning). The implication of being called "Light of the world" is the fact that the Church is meant to give light in a dark world. Conflict darkens the world and confuses the identity of the Church. It basically destroys relationship (cited Dajwan 2018).

d. PEACE:

The Bible mentions the word 'peace' 348 times. Indeed, God Himself is the Author of Peace. Peace is one of the fruit of The Holy Spirit (Gal. 5:22). Peace can be experienced by a believer, true Peace is widely viewed as an absence of dissension, violence, or war.

Galtung's typologies of Peace :

- Negative peace- mere cessation of hostilities
- Positive peace- structural peace; sustainable peace
- Cultural peace- peace due to inculcation of peace virtues, norms or cultural values. (Obadiah Samuel, 2017).

Best (2006) conceptualized peace in the following ways:

Peace as the converse of war:

There is a tendency in peace and conflict studies to conceptualize peace as the converse of war. In other words, peace is defined as the absence of war, and by logical extension, war is the absence of peace. This way of conceptualizing peace though attractive, is inadequate for understanding the nature of peace.

In the **first** place, it is tautological and circular in logic- there is peace because there is no war and there is war because there is no peace. **Second**, it really tells us nothing about the meaning of peace, which, going by this definition, we have to arrive at by first defining war. However, even common sense would suggest that peace does exist independent of war. Thus, there can be peace even when there is war, as in situations when there are peaceful interactions between countries that are engaged in active war. For instance, the Palestinians and Israelis have been able to establish peaceful use of water resources, even as the war between them has raged.

Third, this definition inapplicable in situations of structural violence, as Johan Galtung calls it. War is only one form of violence, which is physical, open and direct. But there is another form of violence that is not immediately perceived as such. This has to do with social conditions such as poverty, exclusion, intimidation, oppression, want, fear and many types of psychological pressure. **Finally**, it would be wrong to classify a country experiencing pervasive structural violence as peaceful. In other words, although war may not be going on in a country where there is pervasive poverty, oppression of the poor by the rich, police brutality, intimidation of ordinary people by those in power, oppression women, or monopolization of resources and power by some sections of the society, it will still be wrong to say that there is peace in such a country. Consequently, it is quite possible not to have peace even when there is no war. Best (2006:3-4).

e. PEACE AND SECURITY:

- Security may be defined as the absence of threats to peace, life and core national values.
- Traditional security perspective- State Centered security
- Human security perspective- human- Centered security- tackling issues of hunger/malnutrition, poverty, unemployment, poor governance, lack of infrastructure etc.

Some Threats to Peace and security;

Generally, threats to peace can come from both State and non-state actors

- **State Actors**- Government e.g. Gadaffi, Idi Amin, Alasad Charles Tailor etc.
- **Non-State Actors**- terroristes, bandits, Drug traffickers, Pirates, kidnappers etc.
- **Other Threats**- Natural disasters, diseases and climate change, among others.

Some specific Threats:

- Armed conflicts
- Structural violence typology
- Injustice
- Bad governance
- Lack of infrastructure/basic needs of life
- Corruption
- Illiteracy
- Poverty
- Unemployment

All the above and many others according to this approach; breeds frustration, which in turn leads to aggression.

Some Challenges for Achieving Sustainable Peace and Security

- Lack of political will to domesticate international conventions and protocols
- Docility of the people towards participatory governance

- Lack of capacity on the part of the people to engage government on issues of public concern- dealing with structural violence
- Corruption and mismanagement of public funds
- Arm Conflicts
- Climate change
- Natural Disasters
- Diseases

f. PEACEBUILDING:

The term "peace building" came into widespread use after 1992 when Boutros-Ghali, the then United Nations Secretary-General announced his agenda for peace (Boutros-Ghali 1992 quoting Lamle Elias). Since then, "peace building" has become a broadly used but often ill-defined term connoting activities that go beyond crisis intervention such as long-term development and building of governance structures and institutions. There are hundreds of organizations today involved in preventing or managing conflict at the international, national and local levels. It has also broadened to include not just armed and resource based conflict, but, poverty, HIV and AIDS (lamle Elias 2015:79). The emphasis of the United Nations has been on structural transformation, with a primary focus on institutional reform. The 2000 report of the panel on United Nations Peace Operations also known as the Brahimi Report refined the definition of peace building as; "Activities undertaken on the far side of conflict to reassemble the foundations of peace and provide the tools for building on those foundations something that is more than just the absence of war" (Brahimi Report 2000).

Indeed, peace building is those activities and programme put in place to address the root cause of conflict, prevent the re-escalation, re-establish democratic structures, and restore relationships and capacity building for sustainable peace and development.

g. PLURALISTIC SOCIETY/COMMUNITY:

Pluralism is one of the main characteristics of contemporary society. Pluralism refers to a situation where more than one thing exists. Likewise religious pluralism is a situation where more than one religious tradition exist and pluralistic society is a situation where by in one community or society there are different kinds of diversities in existence and the different people of that society are conscious of such differences. (Imo, 2005).The Church has a great task/mission and role to play in promoting peaceful co-existence in a pluralistic society. The genuineness of such diversity is attested by the convergent and complementary findings of disciplines such as ethnology, sociology, theology, history and geography. Investigation carried out in these different fields of study reveal striking information about the kind of diversity that exists in the way people decide the organization of community life, the exercise of power, the division of property, the transmission of knowledge and skills as well as cultural and religious expressions. Since human beings have travelled and come in contact with societies other than their own, they have been forced to recognize the immense variety of actual responses which human groups have offered and are still offering to the specific challenging situations they face within their given environments.

The apparently irreducible diversity of the social experiences and expressions by which human groups actually live is an unavoidable fact.

03 THEORITICAL FRAMEWORKS:

It is impossible to identify a single theory that provides construct and frameworks which adequately explain the relationship between religion and peace in any given society/community. Theoretical postulations on this subject are diverse with each strand providing its unique explanation of the complex issue. **Primordialism** views religious strife as the climates of strain in relationships as a result of cultural, identity and historical differences. Ancient hatreds create diverging interest and it is possible for conflict to take place over or between two civilizations. **Instrumentalism** is a political economy approach. It explains the politicization of religion and religious identities and the radicalization of religious communities in response to political and economic decline (Hansenclever and Rittberger, 2000). One of the most influential theses is the one emphasizing that global religious resurgence is currently taking place. Conflict entrepreneurs normally take advantage of this to mobilize groups into violence using religion as the fuel. **Fundamentalism** has to do with extreme beliefs. According to Josie Lebile Holo (2000), extreme believes breed extreme radicalism borne out of gradual processes of dis-education and brainwashing. Most groups that have been branded terrorists use brainwash and dis-educate for recruitment (Gwamma and Panyil, 2011). Brainwashed people constitute a threat to the globe's security. **Action- Reaction theory:** This theory highlights the spontaneous reaction of one group to the threatening acts of another. When the activities of one group engender suspicion and therefore a similar reaction from another based on the assumption that the gains of one amounts to the losses of another (Best, 2011).

On the other hand the **Functionalist perspective** of religion as the personification of human ideals (peace, forgiveness, love, tolerance, contentment, respect, honesty, humility and care for the needy integrity etc). The expectation is for Christians, Muslims and African Traditional Religion practitioners to tap from valuable resources in their holy books, godly human values or practices as the case may be for the common good of their societies/communities. Closely related to this is the **Religious Market Place theory** which proposes that religious freedom engenders by peace by reducing religious related conflicts. The theory projects the importance of positive contribution of religious practices in reducing social evils, especially corruption, which is key impediment to economic development (Grim, 2014). Encouragement on building more on our commonalities like; schools, football/games, hospitals, businesses as in marketing, politics and so on. This is a strand of social theory and religion which got its most compassion arguments from British Sociology, James A. Beckford. These theories are in no way exhaustive. However they provide a framework for most of the arguments in this paper presentation.

04. THE NEXUS BETWEEN RELIGION AND VIOLENCE:

The relationship or the connection of religion and violence is here by briefly explored for our understanding of this paper. According to (Lamle, 2015) asserts First, if we accept the idea that some religions are inherently violent, while others are inherently peaceful, that would mean that there is something within them (i.e. sacred texts, rituals, dogmas or doctrines) that makes them more violent and more peaceful than others. Under these circumstances, we would expect some religions to be in constant state of war, while others would be in a state of permanent peace. That is not the case, however because Christianity that is seen as a peaceful religion you some time discovered its ministers of the gospel fighting each other (Genesis 13:1-8). History shows that every religion was or still is involved in conflicts throughout the world- not only monotheistic religions, because of their belief in the existence of only one true God, as many people seem to believe, but polytheistic ones, too. Despite their belief in a multitude of gods, polytheistic religions do not seem to be more tolerant or peaceful. For instance, in Sri Lanka, Buddhists and Hindus fought each other for decades. In India, the Hindus and Sikhs also confront each other in violent episodes and Hindus and Muslims confront each other in India as well as in Pakistan. Every religion presents some concepts; religious writings or principles that can be used in order to justify the appeal to violence. In Sri Lanka, for instance, although the conflict between the Sinhalese and Tamils is purely political, both the Hindu Tamil minority and the Sinhalese Buddhist majority use their sacred text in order to justify their violent acts against their opponents and to gain political advantages.

Undoubtedly, there are verses both in the Bible and the Quran that can be used for radical and violent interpretations. In this regard Rev.Dr Dachomo in one of his paper in workshops analyzed and said the Meca's Surahs are more of the New testament in the sense of the emphasis on love and peace while Medina's Surahs are more of the Old Testament with emphasis trace of wars example God commanded Joshua and the Israelites to go and kill and conquer Nations (Joshua 8:1ff-1"Then the Lord said to Joshua, "Do not be afraid; do not be discouraged. Take the whole army with you, and go up and attack Ai. For I have delivered into your hands the king of Ai, his people, his city and his land. 2 You shall do to Ai and its king as you did to Jericho and its king, except that you may carry off their plunder and livestock for yourselves. Set an ambush behind the city..." also Chilton in Lamle lecture notes "PCS 513 Religion, Conflict and Peace 2015", focused on the Old Testament story of Abraham and Isaac, a key episode for Jews, Christian and Muslims alike, when God asked Abraham to sacrifice his son, Isaac, but at last moment, because Abraham had proved his faith, being prepared to slain his son, God stopped him and pointed out a ram caught in a thicket as a sacrifice to substitute Isaac. He also argues that, although the true and original meaning of the story is that human sacrifice is not desired by God (Hebrews 10:1-10), all the three monotheisms have altered the meaning of the story in times of persecution, glorifying martyrdom. **Quran** also contains verses such as this: 'And when the sacred months are passed, kill those who join other gods with God wherever you shall find them; and seize them, besiege them, and lay wait for them with every kind of ambush'. But the Surah continues as this: 'yet if they repent, and take to prayer, and render the purifying dues, let them go their way: for, behold, God is much forgiving, a dispenser of grace.' And then continues like this: 'If any those who ascribe divinity to aught beside God seeks thy protection, grant him protection, so that he might [be able to] hear the word of God [from thee]; and thereupon convey him to a place where he can feel secure: this, because they [may be] people who [sin only because they] do not know [the truth]'. And although the most feared concept of Islam is 'jihad', the interpretation of Jihad as war against the infidels is just one of the meanings of the term which also mean an inner struggle against evil temptations for wrong doing, as a way to get closer to God and to achieve the inner peace. For many centuries, Muslims lived in peace with their neighbors, without waging holy war against them. Moreover, there are millions of Muslims that still live in peace with their neighbors and do not feel compelled by their scriptures to run jihad, in the bellicose sense of the concept. Even in the wake of the tragic events of 11 September; Muslim scholars and leaders worldwide condemned the terrorist attacks and declared that terrorists distort Islam.

On the other hand, there are some unconditionally peaceful **Christian denominations** (like Quakers and Jehovah's witnesses, for instance, who refuse to touch any kind of arms), who guide their social life according to Jesus' words: 'But I tell you, do not resist-an evil person. If someone strikes you on the right cheek, turn to him the other also' (Matthew 5:39). The **Anabaptist tradition** is also built upon the idea that all kind of violence is prohibited by the Bible and takes the words of Jesus: 'Blessed are the peacemakers, for they shall be4 called children of God' (Matthew 5:9) literally, considering that those who promote War under any circumstances are not genuine Christians. However, they very same Christianity has produced the just war doctrine according to which under certain circumstances, war can be pursued. **We can deduce,** therefore, that the interpretative apparatus of each religion is very important when we discuss religions' involvement in violent actions. It is obvious that Osama bin Laden's aggressive interpretation of Islam is considerably different than the moderates' interpretations, just as the Christianity's Holy Scriptures are differently interpreted by different Christian denominations or persons. Therefore, we cannot affirm that Islam, Judaism or Christianity, or any other religion is inherently violent by concentrating on isolated texts from the Holy Scriptures- the interpretative apparatus make the difference in each case. The interpretation of the sacred scriptures by some radical religious leaders calling for violent combat against the infidels is just one interpretation amongst others. The diversity that exists within each of the religious traditions has to be considered in order to avoid biased conclusions (Lamle 2015).

Secondly, in considering the nexus between religion and violence, there is need to analyzes the relationship between religion and violence it is imperative to avoid the trap of considering our own religion in idealistic terms, by taking into account only the peaceful paragraphs and ideas of our sacred Scriptures, while considering other religions through the lenses of its extremists' acts of terror and violence. Researchers' subjectivism is often responsible for errors in analyzing the involvement of religion in conflict. When analyzing the relationship between religion and violence it is imperative to consider the **particular context** in which certain interpretations of the sacred texts emerge. The context in which a religious group finds itself determines which aspect of a religious tradition is given preeminence and is used. The excessive use of collocations such as the 'Islamic terrorism' or the 'war against terrorism', which has in view only the Muslim communities and no other religious terrorist networks like the Tamil, the IRA or the ETA, for instance, could foster radical interpretations of Islam, by discontented Muslims who may very well perceive themselves as being under siege, and thus the call for a jihad against the infidels to defend Allah's community may find more supporters than under ordinary conditions (Lamle 2015).

Discrimination (which can be political, cultural, social, economic or religious-remember the functions of religion) against a religious tradition or against a religious minority determines that minority to form **grievances** over this discrimination, it would be wrong to classify a country experiencing pervasive **structural violence as peaceful**. In other words, although war may not be going on in a country where there is pervasive poverty, oppression of the poor by the rich, police brutality, intimidation of ordinary people by those in power, oppression women, or monopolization of resources and power by some sections of the society, it will still be wrong to say that there is peace in such a country. Consequently, it is quite possible not to have peace even when there is no war. Best (2006:3-4). These grievances determine the minority group to mobilize and there is a great probability that mobilized groups take part in conflicts. This is certainly the case in Sri Lanka, for instance, where the discriminatory policies of the Sinhalese majority determine violent reactions from the Tamils and contribute, thus, to a circle of an endless violence. One of the most important things when analyzing the relationship between religion and violence is therefore to make a distinction between religion as a metaphysical and ethical system and politicized religion as anti-system revolt presented in a religious garb and legitimated in a religious language. **Taking** as a case study the violent acts perpetrated by some of the Muslims in Europe, for instance, **Olivier Roy** argued that there is in fact nothing like an Islamic element in such violent acts. When Muslims go to the streets, they are actually driven by the frustration of not being integrated enough and their riots are actually a call for a better integration within the western societies from which they are alienated and which do not meet their expectations.

In the global context, the attraction of the radical Islamism is not surprising, given the fact that the Muslim world feel that it is denied a decent place within the global system, which is run by non-Muslims, while it lives in constant fight with poverty, famine, illiteracy and decayed infrastructures. **The analysis of the specific context of each so-called religious-based conflict would most probably prove that the causes and the stakes of those conflicts are more political, structural and geographical than religious.** When analyzing the relation between religion and violence it is also important to consider that during the last decades an important religious transformation took place under the influence of the globalization forces. **Globalization** has created a favorable context for religion to become more 'democratic', in the sense that the individuals and groups increasingly think for themselves and contest the role of the formal religion and of the religious authority and become directly responsible to God rather than to 'man made' religious institutions. In other words, religion becomes increasingly distanced from the religious hierarchy and thus less 'institutionalized', decision-making becoming the appanage of the individual or of the small groups. According, as Otis observes, 'individuals and groups on all continents and in all social strata have begun constructing a new religious politics based on the relationship between a transcendent being and themselves- bypassing or redefining traditional forms of state/church authority. **The new reality is the emergence of particularistic do-i- yourself religion(s),** in which some individuals use a peculiar form of logic to perpetuate violence in order to fulfill what they believe is God's will. Thus, the structure of violence and warfare in the modern world… is violence perpetuated by individuals on the global stage in pursuit of transcendent goals- **albeit** by earthly means'. Accordingly, the terrorist acts are individual acts, not acts endorsed by the institutionalized traditional religious communities. [**Ninety nine percent of terrorists are Muslims but not all Muslims are terrorists**].

Although individuals pertaining to all religions can be and sometimes are engaged in violent conflicts, their acts are hardly the result of those religions' theologies. As **Mark Juergensmeyer**- one of the leading experts in religious violence today- argued, the terrorist acts in the name of religion are acts of individuals which believe that there is a grave social injustice in the world, which is an offence against God and that any action on His behalf against those responsible for this injustice is approved by God. Under these circumstances, I contend that no religious tradition as a whole can be blamed for violent acts perpetrated by groups or individuals. Nor Islam or Christianity, nor Judaism or Buddhism, nor Hinduism or Sikhism is inherently violent, nor are they inherently peaceful. Not all the Muslims are violent, just as not all the Christians or the Jews or the Hindus or the Sikhs, for example, are violent; and certainly, not all of them are always peaceful. Distinctions and nuances are to be made in each case when analyzing the nexus between religion violence (Lamle 2015).

The nexus between religion and security; in analyzing this, it is essential to consider also the positive contributions of religion to stability and security. It is true that religion is often politicized and can serve as a tool in the hands of the warring parties, but religion is also significant element in the management. It can be noted that religious actors have been key players in many conflicts around the world, (the Mangu and Bokkos friction of 1994/1995) and they have made an essential contribution to the conflict prevention, the peaceful resolution of the differences, the mediation of the conflicts and the reconciliation of the conflicting parties, due to their unique set of **moral values and beliefs that can motivate changes of attitude and action.** In this respect, and drawing from the field experience of some of these religious actors, some authors promote faith-based diplomacy as an essential form of diplomacy especially in those situations that involve communal (predominantly religious) identities for which traditional diplomacy is not enough prepared. The concept of faith- based diplomacy was popularized by Douglas Johnston. This kind of diplomacy relies on virtues, discourses and practices of different religious tradition as essential components of diplomacy and although it is a rather new type of diplomacy, it is already a part of the training of diplomats in the US and will probably soon be introduced by other countries, too. **The introduction of the spiritual dimension** in the conflict management efforts is very important, one reason for that being the fact that a significant part of the human conflicting behavior is based on emotional feelings that cannot be changed by negotiations, dialogue, mediation and rational bargaining; accordingly, the use of the spiritual/religious element can make actors to critically examine their actions and attitudes. According to the supporters of the faith-based diplomacy and the experience has already proved the religious and as the religious leaders and institutions, and the religious based NGOs are best trained for this kind of diplomacy. As Thomas argue in Lamle, the religious actors are particularly well placed to act as mediators, provide a 'neutral' space for negotiations, because they are respected for the set of values they represent and promote, they know very well the local problems, they enjoy credibility and trust, they have the ability to mobilize national and international support for the peace process and they have the possibility to employ such spiritual elements like the prayer or other religious rituals that can represent efficient means in the process of healing and reconciliation. Also, their legitimacy allows them to reach out to the parties in conflict, especially at times when the other diplomats and Track One actors fail to. A case studies of some of faith-based organizations foundation in Plateau state of Nigeria

St. Egidio Community was actively involved in the peace process in Mozambique, Burundi, Congo and Kosovo, using a Catholic-inspired approach. **Monsignor Jaime Goncalves, archbishop of Beira**, had an important contribution in the peace agreement in Mozambique, in 1992, an agreement that put an end to a war that had cost millions of lives and determined half of the population to flee. In Zaire, **Monsignor Laurent Monsengwo** has played a crucial role during the negotiations between president Mobutu and his opponents. A crucial role was played by the religious actors in Nicaragua in the 80s, as well as in the end of the apartheid in South Africa and also in the collapse of the communism in some Eastern European countries. Religious for peace has successfully mediated the conflict in Sierra Leone and contributed to the creation of a reconciliation climate in Bosnia and Kosovo. **The Quakers** (The Religious Society of Friends) were involved in the mediation of the conflict in Sri-Lanka. The Mennonites have created the Mennonite Conciliation Service in the late 70s, the Christian Peacemaker Teams and the international Conciliation Service and through these institutions they were actively engaged in the reconciliation efforts between the Sunnis and the Shia in Iraq and activated in South Africa, from the 70s until the end of the apartheid. In South Africa, a special importance had the truth and reconciliation commissions, which proved the force of religion in overcoming hostility and antagonisms. **The Plowshares Institute**, created by the Methodists, has trained religious leaders for actions of peace building throughout the world, based on a spiritual and moral approach. **The World Conference on Religion and Peace** is the biggest international coalition formed by the representatives of all the major world religions, dedicated to maintaining peace in the world. It is currently present on all continents and in the worst conflict areas of the world, trying to create multi-religious partnerships to mobilize the moral and spiritual resources of religious people, in order to resolve their mutual problems (Lamle 2015).

There are many other religious organizations besides the already mentioned ones that incorporated the principles of the faith-based diplomacy: among them the

- American Friends Service Committee,
- The Catholic Relief Services,
- The Center for the Study of Islam and Democracy,
- The European Platform for Conflict Prevention and Transformation,
- The Life and Peace Institute,
- TEKAN Peace Desk,
- The Mennonite Central Committee,
- The Mercy Corps International,
- The Religion and Peacemaking Program,
- The World Council of Churches,
- The International Islamic Forum for Dialogue,
- Conflict and Peacebuilding etc.

05. USE OF RELIGION FOR THE CREATION OF VIOLENCE (CHALLENGES) IN AFRICA

i. USE OF RELIGION FOR CREATION OF VIOLENCE IN AFRICA: PRIMORDIALISM/ACTION-REACTION THEORY

Perhaps out of the desire to be politically correct some have wished away the primordial issues that laid the foundation for the use of religion to create conflict in Africa. According to Turakin (2012), it is not possible for Africa to have a proper grasp of the nature of religious and communal clashes, frictions, riots, conflicts and violence without understanding our primordial, religious, cultural and colonial past; what we were before the arrival of Islam, colonial masters and Christian missions, and what we become during and after the Islamic, Colonial, Christian and post-colonial era.

Since Arab expansion in the eight century and European expansion in the fifteenth century, Africans have almost completely converted from their indigenous, traditional religions to Christianity and Islam. This situation was compounded by the colonialists who petitioned the country into different entities for administrative convenience at the Berlin Conference of 1884/1885. The religious and socio cultural dynamics off the continent was not taken into consideration. The result is what primordialists such as Huntington (1993) called the "Clash of Civilizations". Huntington submitted that while the struggle of ideologies stopped after the cold war, the world had only reverted to a normal state of affair characterized by cultural conflicts.

In the West African country Sudan, Christians and African Traditional Religion practitioners in the southern region of the country have fought the central government controlled by Muslims to a standstill until they secured the independence of South Sudan in July 2010. Since Sudan's independence of 1956, only 10 out of those 58 years have been peace. In 1947, despite religious and cultural differences, the British and Egyptian colonizers decided to make Sudan on country. This is led to the first civil war, which lasted from 1955-1972. Again around 1983-2005, a second war erupted between the north and south. The war in Dafur took off in 2003 when rebel forces took up arms, accusing the government of unfair practices.

There are many explanations to the years of conflict in Sudan which seemingly ended with independence of South Sudan in 2010 as we shall observe later. However, fundamental to the crises was the unequal yoking of the black Christian/African Traditional worshippers of South and the Arab Muslim of the north. However, there are fundamental issues related to the conflict in Sudan which this theory cannot sufficiently explain as we shall later observe. In Nigeria the Christian and Muslim population are almost equal in number. The majority of Nigerian Muslims are concentrated in the north, while the Christians are concentrated in the South and Middle Belt. Nigeria was relatively harmonious and stable. But from 1980s, the country began to experience religious unrest and violence. It started with Maitasine movement in northern Nigeria in December 1980. There was also the Kafanchan, Kaduna and Zaria, Zangon Kataf, Gwantu and other parts of Kaduna State(intermittently from 1987) [the story of Bishop Kukah during eating] Tafawa Balewa and other parts of Bauchi State(intermittently from 1991); Jos metropolis and other parts of Plateau State (intermittently 1994). This is in addition to violence in the northern states against the implementation of the Sharia Law legal system in 2000. This dimension of violence with religious connotations continued in 2009, when the Islamic group Boko Haram began an armed rebellion against the government and Christians. The conflict has spiraled into a more violent phase to date. Most of the conflicts are between Christian/African Traditional Religion practitioners and Muslims, except in the case of Islamic fundamentalist groups, Boko Haram and Maitasine (Best, Mwangvat and Gwamna and Gamaliel, 2011).

While there perhaps several reasons to explain the conflicts experienced in Nigeria, it cannot be denied that the bases for some of the conflict were primordial. The violence which followed protest against the implementation of the Sharia legal system is a good case in point. While Christians saw the implementation as outrageous and an infringement of their religious freedom in a circular state, Muslims saw Sharia as an integral aspect of their worship. It was indeed a stalemate! According to Ochonu (2014), clashes between Muslims and Christians in Nigeria has become as daily affair:

In Nigeria's National politics, Christian anxieties about Muslim Domination of the national political space and the accompanying fear that politically dominant Muslims would use their privilege to Islamize national institution and impose the Sharia legal law on non- Muslims date back as old as Colonial times. Muslim on their part especially those from the Northern Nigeria, for their part, have sought to fend off what they regard as Unbridled Westernization and have sporadically sought refuge in religious reforms (Ochonu, 2014).

Although the central African Republic has no history of sectarian conflict of deep religious tension, the United Nations has recently been warning that the CAR is facing wide spread religions violence that could take genocidal proportions. According to Washington times, the conflict became increasingly religious when members of the Seleka rebel coalition looted, raped and killed Christians upon seizing control of the capital city in Banjul 201. This speaks of how the Action/ Reaction tensions between the two religions have continued to fuel tensions in different parts of the continent.

ii. USE OF RELIGION FOR THE CREATION OF CONFLICT IN AFRICA: INSTRUMENTALISM

In spite of the validity of the primordial approach in explaining the violence in Africa; it is insufficient in addressing all these conflicts and several others in Africa. Instrumentalism explores deeper to explain how political interests use religion as an instrument of realizing their political and economic ambitions. Most of what is referred to clash of civilization in Africa is actually clash of interest.

Take the case of Southern Sudan, since independence 2010, the country has been handicapped by competing interest of powerful political actors and the interests they represent. The country is still facing massive state- corroding corruption, political instability within the ruling party, Sudan People's Liberation Movement and tensions with Sudan over the sharing of oil revenues. On December 15th 2013, tensions between factions loyal to President Salva Kir, of Dinker ethnic group, and those aligned with the former Vice President, Riek Machar, of the Nuer ethnic group, exploded into fighting on the streets of the capital city Juba. Southern Sudan's dramatic return to war has torn communities apart and left thousands dead. In September 2014, 1.8 Million people were still afraid to return to their homes (Conflict in Sudan: Southern Sudan: The World's newest country in www.enoughproject.org). Therefore it is too simplistic to say the conflict between Sudan and South Sudan was a purely Muslim verse Christian affair or purely based on primordial issues.

Another flash point of violence with religious in Africa is Kenya. The port of Mombasa Kenya's second largest city is at the center of a religious divide. It is a predominantly Muslim region of an otherwise Christian nation, and residents of the area often complain of government neglect. Their tensions have often erupted in to violence. Such instances include street battles between police and Islamic groups in 1992 and recent attacks by unidentified gunmen at strategic spots in the country, the West Gate in Nairobi the capital city. Since the West Gate attack by Somalian Islamist group al-shabaab, Kenya conflict began in 1982, in Mombasa between the police and supporters of the Islamic Party in Kenya, which was trying to get its members elected into parliament on a radical agenda. West seem obvious was that politicians on both sides of the divide were protecting their interests.

Even the implementation of the Sharia legal system in Northern Nigeria which led to violence in 2000 was not a clash of civilizations. It seems Muslim politicians in Northern Nigeria, led by former Governor of Zamfara State Ahmad Sani Yarima, found a cheap way of attaining popularity by capitalizing on a popular sentiment in the region. Christian politicians on the other hand responded with the same measure of political dexterity, referring to the implementation of Sharia as an integral part of the grand plan to Islamize the country. No doubt, both Christian and Muslim leaders made good returns from these crises at the expense of their followers and the conflict continues.

iii. USE OF RELIGION FOR THE CREATION OF CONFLICT IN AFRICA: FUNDAMENTALISM

It has been argued that Iranian revolution of 1979 led by Ayattolah Khomeni provided great impetus for the contemporary rise of Islamic fundamentalism. The revolution provided renewed interest in the purification of Islam (Tamuno, 1991). Curiously, the Maitasine upraising in Northern Nigeria began in 1980. According to Kadala, however, the firm establishment of Islam in the north is attributed to the jihad of Usman Dan Fodio in the nineteenth century. This was a reformation of Islamic principles. Dan Fodio was a Muslim cleric who was appalled at the syncretistic behavior of the Hausa rulers. He was born to the Torankawa Fulani family in 1754, and was brought up as a member of the Sunni sect of Islam. He was of the Kadariyya Fraternity, which according to Johnson was the oldest and most widespread of the Islamic orders. He preached against syncretism and this brought about tension between him and the ruler of Gobir, leading to some limited skirmishes between him and Yunfa the king of Gobir. This later metamorphosed into a full-fledged jihad. This reformation eventually came to be known as the Fulani jihad. Indeed the news of this jihad spread to other parts of the north; therefore, Fulani people from various parts of the north came to Gobir and collected jihad flags, which they used to launch the jihad in their various areas. For instance, in Fombina (in the south of Borno Empire) known today as Adamawa region, the Fulani of this region were already in constant conflict with their local indigenous rulers. So Modibo Adama from Fombina went to Sokoto and received a flag from Usman Dan Fodio, and launched the jihad in Fombina and established the Adamawa Emirate in what is now Taraba state. Yakubu from Bauchi, a former student of Dan Fodio, established the Bauchi Emirate. Buba Yero took the green flag from Dan Fodio and established the Gombe Emirate.

Fundamentalism is however not an entire Muslim phenomenon as it is being erroneously perceived in some quarters. There are Christians sects in Africa sects that teach their followers that being suspicious of Muslims is a virtue. Muslims are referred to as Ishmaelite's who are violent by nature. Thus during conflicts, there is an unwritten law that says, "Muslims are violent people who should be killed". This is the reality seen in most so called Christian/African Traditional Religion Practitioners verses Muslims, especially here in Jos Nigeria, the Plateau State capital which has been in and out of conflict from 1994 to date. It is important to note the Muslim verse Muslim dimension of most fundamental movements in Africa. For instance, the Boko Haram movement in Nigeria uses a literalist reading of the Islamic text for recruitment. They stressed the belief to recreate a golden Islamic age of the past. They believe the failure of the Muslim world is rooted in the failure of Muslims themselves (Mangvwat, 2011). Therefore, their attacks are targeted both non- Muslims and Muslims.

The fundamentalist model of using religion to create violence is not peculiar to the Boko Haram. Most global groups that use the name of Islam to pursue socio political and economic agenda have over the years employed this old trick to recruit members towards projecting their agenda. In Mali, several Islamic groups, led by Tuareg-based National Movement for the liberation of Azawad (MNLA) rebelled against the Malian government (16th January, 2012). This instigated a military take- over by the military of President Toure (March, 2012). The rebels however took control of the north in April, 2012. By June, 2012, the Islamic group that partnered with the Tuareq took over and established a fundamentalist form of sharia law. They remained in power until the Malian government called to France to launch an intervention in 2013.

It is however important to note that the Tuaregs never desired the implementation of Sharia of Islamic Law when they began the rebellion in January, 2012; what they wanted was an independent state in which they could protect their culture. However, the up raising was hijacked by fundamentalist (Peter Chilson, in Atlanta Blackstar 2014). In Uganda, rebels of the Lord's Resistance Army have conducted a civil war in the north of the country which has spread to several parts of East Africa. Their goal is a Christian Theocracy in Uganda whose laws are based on the biblical Ten Commandments (Religious Tolerance, Ontario Canada www.religioustolerance.org). LRA leader Joseph Kony, who often speaks in Messianic tones claims to be the savior of the Acholi, the population has nonetheless been subjected to mindless atrocities at the whim of the leader by his own divine struck. (History and Heritage Travel in Africa. Peterbeterafrica.com) [President Mahammadu Buhari is an example of fundamentalist who in one of campaigns words said a Muslim should vote a Muslim and he fails in 2011].

06. THE AFRICAN TRADITIONAL RELIGION AND CONFLICT

The presenter has earlier alluded to the premise that most Africa has been converted into Christianity or Islam religions. However, there remains a fraction of practitioners of the indigenous faith in the continent. The practitioners of the indigenous faith are cut up in a complex web during crises that bear components of the Muslim verse Christian rivalry. No doubt, they align with their interests during conflicts.

Curiously, adherents of the two religions turn to the practitioners of the African faith for "powers" in form of charms for protection. Therefore, the indigenous faith is used during conflict to give confidence for the two parties. Perhaps it is safe to hazard the theory the confidence Muslims or Christians receive from the protection powers of the African Traditional Religion or "black power" provides some form of energy, whether real or unreal, which fuels and sustains conflict in the continent.

Extracts from a letter by King Leopold of Belgium to Christian missionaries in Congo in 1883 gives impetus to this postulation:

> *Reverends, Fathers, and Dear Compatriot .... Your principal objective in our mission is never to teach the niggers to know God, this they know already.... Your essential task*

is to facilitate the task of administrators and industrialist.... You have to detach from them and disrespect everything that gives them courage to affront us. I make reference to their mystic and their war fetish- war protection-...you must do every in your power to make it disappear.

According to Best (2011), most conflicts emanate from deep historical narrations by parties of the conflict. Some communities believe themselves to be warriors from history. Such images are brought into their present relationships. During conflicts their goal is to win to justify that past. Indeed, conflict will be hard and difficult to get to the end because each party is aiming at winning.

07. HOW RELIGION COULD BE ENGAGED IN THE MANAGEMENT OF CONFLICT (OPPORTUNITIES):

In considering Christianity, Islam and African Traditional Religion to conflict resolution and this is rooted in the biblical values and godly human values;

> *Since most world religions have peace entrenched in their Holy books, religion can easily be used as instrument for peace education among persons as well as other adherents and followers. Members of different faiths should one another's' opinion and religious beliefs. There should be respect for the diversity of religions. Religions should respect and promote the virtues of peace, forgiveness, reconciliation, love, respect for life and other values that promote non- violent change (Gumut 2006:165).*

a. CHRISTIAN APPROACHES TO CONFLICT MANAGEMENT

Fundamentalism in Christianity is not a familiar theme in our contemporary world. However, this study is not oblivious of the fundamentalist stands associated with the LRA in East Africa and the well documented stories of the crusaders in Europe and Asia and the so called Catholics verse Protestant debacle in Northern Ireland in Europe, which was brought to a climax by the Good Friday peace accord. Therefore we humbly distance ourselves from the common bigotry which suggests that only Muslim groups use violence as means to an end.

However, there is a need to present a unique approach on how to use Christianity for the promotion of peace in the continent. This must also begin by addressing the popular primordial concept of Christians as victims who are being hunted down by Jihadists; hence Christians are only responding, fire for fire. The so called Action- Reaction Model which some Christian leaders cum politicians have told their followings to pursue out of necessity should be identified as the fallacy it is. Christians give up this notion from their hearts to begin to increasingly seek for more constructive ways of resolving tensions/conflicts, [**the need to learn from King David in the book of 1Samuel 30:1-8; David's responses- Distress-A. Inward focus;-B. Upward focus-asks God; C. Forward focus-action and Genesis 13:1-8 Abraham and Lot's Herdsmen**].

McCain (2011) made some useful suggestions in this direction when he maintained that any Christian blueprint for conflict resolution that does not respect the convictions of the non- Christian and does not include inputs from all parts of the society will not succeed. The best way to break down negative stereotypes and create peace in the community is to interact as freely as possible with others from different backgrounds (**dialogue with people of other faiths as in Acts 6:1-7 desensitization and deliberation-need to focus on the ministry of the word and prayers- Dr Dachomo Illustration about if you wake up and discovered you are just the one living; if all people have accepted Christ then there is no need for the great commission or dialogue**). And because God has given to everyone a choice, Christians must recognize and respect that choice (McCain, 2011).

During conflicts supporting the victims of disaster is consistent with the provisions of the Bible. This should in form of relief to those affected on both sides. This will greatly promote peaceful coexistence. Most conflicts in Africa that have religious components are compounded with the settler indigene nomenclature. This is however alien to the provisions of the Bible which commands adherents never to mistreat aliens or foreigners who live among them. Aliens had the right to grow rich in the land of Israel and even obtain Jewish slaves. Indeed, the Biblical values are models for engaging religion in bringing peace in Africa, Nigeria and Plateau State Leviticus 25:47 (Dajwan 2016).

b. ISLAMIC APPROACHES TO CONFLICT MANAGEMENT

No doubt Islam is the worst hit in terms its perception by non- adherents as a religion that promotes violence. Muslim criminals who commit crimes are branded Islamic fundamentalists. The Western press shares some blame for how Islam is being perceives, but the blame is not entirely theirs. Politicians and bad elements among Muslims have used religion to pursue personal interests through a literalist misinterpretation of the concept of Jihad to naïve followers.

However, the Qur'an offers a deep reservoir for conflict management. There are pacifist positions embedded in Islamic teachings. This should be harnessed for the common good of all in the continent. Muslims have laudable records of good neighborliness in African in terms of morality. For instance, during the Rwanda genocide, the Muslim Tutsi population of Rwanda and Burundi did not participate in the wars (Abdulla, 2006). Historical misuses, abuses, and misinterpretations of Islamic sources have diluted the strong emphasis of the religion on justice, equality and freedom (2006).

Exploring provisions of the Qur'an on religious plurality is a perfect point to being addressing the primordial factors responsible for the conflicts associated to the religion. The Qur'an acknowledges plurality in human society in a positive way. The Qur'an views plurality as a sign of God's compassion and mercy. Muslim should by extension acknowledge the multiplicity of language, tribe and colour by embracing co-existence (Abubakar, 2011). Engaging the community in the intervention and resolution processes is also another integral aspect of Islam that is important to this discussion. The Islamic theory and culture emphasize a strong sense of community-have have a lot differences within their sects/denominations but when it comes to a common agenda they are one as in sense of community (Abdullah, 2006) as in Dajwan 2016.

c. AFRICAN APPROACHES TO CONFLICT MANAGEMENT

African Traditional Religion is deeply intertwined with the culture and tradition of the people. They are Siamese twins in all African societies. Even though the practices may vary from one community/

society to the other, the religion is based on familiar, openness/transparency, participation, peaceful co-existence, respect, tolerance, communality, love, forgiveness and humility, among others. The methods and processes of conflict resolution in most African societies are deeply rooted in these principles/values mentioned above (Osei- Hwedie and Morena, 2010).

The presenter therefore submit that: Africans must rediscover the values embedded in their customs and traditions which capture the collective knowledge and experiences of the people especially values like; African value of communality, universal of human family, helping the needy, social relationship and dignity of hard work among others. This is possible if stakeholders in peace are increasingly guided by these values towards resolving contemporary conflicts in the continent. In Rwanda, the justice in the grass community justice system otherwise referred to as Gacaca, which is based on these cherished African values were used in the aftermath of the genocide in the prosecution of hundreds of thousands of perpetrators of crimes against humanity. The results have been remarkably positive (Lamle, 2015). These Alternative Dispute Resolution techniques should increasingly be used to resolve conflicts in the continent.

Lamle (2015) gave examples of similar courts for African Traditional Conflict Mediation Processes to include the Kotga-Botswana, the Dare- Zambabwe, Mato- oput- Northern Uganda. According to him, the Traditional Conflict Mediation Processes are important in contemporary African societies because they effectively address inadequacies of Western courts to effectively address cases of conflicts. These African approaches lay emphasis on forgiveness, communality, love, restoration and reconciliation against punishment. They are also less costly (Lamle, 2015).

Another important example is the concept of Ubuntu embedded in the religion and tradition of most African society. It is a concept that discourages unhealthy rivalry and competition that leads to jealousy, tension, and strife. Most Africans with rural backgrounds may not know the word Ubuntu as the concept is referred to in South Africa, but they are not oblivious of the philosophies of the concept.

> *African people recognize the diversity that exists in what they perceive as truth, thereby giving them the ability to read better meanings in their conflict. At the same time it opens their minds into understanding that they are not actually victims. These help them to stop demonizing others (Lamle 2015).*

The concept of I am because we are! In addition, conflict resolution in Africa involves spiritual practices such as curses, witchcraft and oath-taking among others. Parties are brought before traditional and spiritual leaders including Priest, custodians of deities and soothsayers. One party may invoke a curse by using the name of a deity to harm another perceived wrong doing. When that happens, it is expected that the other party will swear on an oath against the claim. However, failure to respond to an oath is perceived to be the admission of guilt (Kendie and Guri, 2006). These practices were internalized by communities in Africa, and are conceptualized to capture the people's collective knowledge and experiences and yield possible result (Osie- Hwedie and Morena, 2010) as in Dajwan 2016.

08. CONCLUSION AND RECOMMENDATIONS

Africa has experienced tragic violent upheavals in the aftermath of colonialism. The influence of colonialism on African cultural values system is doubtlessness. Colonialism stimulated positive and negative changes in Africa. More importantly, colonial rule was an imposition that unleashed deadly blow on African culture with the immediate consequence of the introduction of such values rugged individualism, corruption, capitalism and oppression. Colonial rule disrupted the traditional machinery of moral homogeneity and practice. The method of moral inculcation was vitiated, which resulted in the abandonment of traditional norms and values through systematic depersonalization of the African and paganisation of its values. Instead of the cherished communalism which defined the life of the African, for example, a burgeoning societal construct was introduced which alienates and destroys the organic fabric of the spirit of We-feeling Ogboin (2011: 101).

In regard of African education Elias Lamle (2016:1) says;

> Notably, African education aimed at developing the total man making him or her responsible members of the community. The curricular includes physical, mental, spiritual and moral development of citizens. The thrust of the Moral education was solidarity. This concept is defined in many African Societies by different terms; some of these terms are 'Ijam', 'ubuntu'and 'ujamaa'.

The anthropological surveys indicate that most African society reveals the fact that socio-political philosophy of traditional African society, hinge on the concept of 'social solidarity and belongingness, and such was ingrained in every citizen from cradle. Regrettable, this social philosophy has been neglected in the modern African. Therefore, he said and I concur that if sanity, peace and Godly values must return to Africa, she must re-introduce or incorporate her biblical and African cultural values and moral system into her educational system, with certain modifications to meet the contemporary church and society of the Africans. The traditional system of education incorporated the ideas of learning skill, social and cultural values and norms into its purpose and method. Hence in African traditional society, the education of her progenies started at birth and continued to adulthood said Lamle (2016:9).

According to Okoduwa (2008:18), colonial rulers promoted their economic and values. This is evident in economic exploitation and socio-religious verification that characterized the colonial period. It is in this theorizing that Irvin Markovitz conceives of colonialism as "one expression of an ever more encompassing capitalism". However, apart from the economic exploitation agenda, colonialism expressed "the ethnocentric belief that the morals and values of the colonizer were superior to those of the colonized". This belief was programmatically achieved through the establishment of schools; example there is schools for the Africans and schools for the white men children-e.g the Hilcreas in Jos Plateau State of Nigeria, which curricula were tailored to achieve the goals of the colonizer rather than train the colonized to be independent and missionary ventures, which helped a great deal in vitrifying the religious concept and inclination of the colonized. This scenario naturally created two classes, one being the superiogatory and the other sub-ordinary, with deliberate administrative structure that favored the former. Even today we experience this ill-treatment among ourselves treating the white special than our fellow Africans Igboin quoting Okoduwa p.18.

One consequence of this was the erosion of the values, culture and religion of the sub-ordinary. The African cosmos became a victim of extraneous ideology which it has continued to grapple with, with little or no success. For instance, as part of the erosion of the African cultural values, Africans now bear at least a European or Christian names (Daniel 1:1-8; changing of names, language, and transformation through food, dresses, businesses and buildings). This means that African names, arts, music, religion etc. are inferior or pagan in orientation and value. The acceptance of this by the Africans has continued to have serious negative effects on the post-colonial Africa and its values.

It must be said that the values discussed above are not exhaustive. It is also necessary to say that African values were not at all times positively adhered to before the coming of the three incursive forces of slave trade, foreign religions (Christianity and Islam) and colonialism. That was why I did said that the three previously have contributed positively and negatively especially in outline number 11. Nevertheless while slave trade abused the sacredness and dignity of human value, some Africans were collaborators, with the foreign religions which led to many changes in African values. Even those values that correspond to the values in these religions in traditional African values were disparaged. For colonialism the political value of African was dislodged and replaced with a foreign one, thus putting a round stick in a square hole. Luke Mbefo argues that combined conspiracy of Christianity and colonialism resulted in the dereliction of African values. I disagree with him because not all Christian dance all through with the philosophy of the colonialism. To most of the African societies these new values have replaced the old values. **What** is responsible for this? The reasons are multi facet; for it is difficult to identify a single variable responsible in any conflict in any given pluralistic society. However in this paper, the presenter has observed that the religious component responsible for some of the most tragic conflicts of the continent has been a reality which cannot be overlooked. These religious factors may include; primordialism, instrumentalism, or fundamentalism; all of which say something about methods aggrieved or selfish individuals within any of the religions (Christianity, Islam and African Traditional Religion) use to incite people to take up arms.

Therefore, conflicts may not be purely religious, however religion is used to fuel and sustain conflicts. Politicians in the continent have a penchant for doing this because it is a cheap way of galvanizing support. However, just as it is unsafe to call a conflict a purely religious matter or a clash of civilizations, it is also unsafe to assume that the religious factors fuelling a conflict are inconsequential. There is a need for a careful approach to handle conflicts bearing religious strands; this is an urgent need considering the fact that conflicts involving values are the most difficult to manage.

Religions in Africa should be used for the transformation of conflicts to positive functions; even when the conflict is not a purely religious matter. Religion is the personification of the highest human ideals of love, peace, generosity as in care for the needy integrity, respect, tolerance, social cohesion and forgiveness. Africa must return to its past of respect for these values. The continent must shun the temptation to be westernized along a path that bears no semblances with these values (the gay marriage debate for instance). After all, Africa became war tone Africa because it lost connection with the values during the years of plunder and scramble for the heart and soul of the continent by Europeans. Again, religion is perhaps the most strategic tool which if rightly harnessed will strangulate social injustice, oppression, cowardice and timidity in international relations policies, corruption and nepotism among other variables responsible for conflicts in our dear pluralistic societies/communities and continent. At this juncture the presenter purses to ask, "Will there be violence in Africa if we all truly adhere to the basic dictates of our faiths"?, (Dajwan 2018).

RECOMMENDATION

Therefore, going through the challenges and opportunities of how religion is used to create conflicts in Africa and how religion can be engage to managing the conflicts in the Continent, the following recommendation is drawn by the presenter:

1. Peace and Security workers, Conflict Managers and the Faith-Based Organizations must strive to erase the popular sentiment of the average man in the Church and on the streets who views religious conflicts from as entirely the end product of primordialism. The people must to be increasingly aware of other salient factors such as the manipulation of religion for selfish ends by those that shape opinion and create the agenda for discussions and debates in the pluralistic society.
2. This article highly recommends tools explained in this work such as (Mbiti), Ubuntu and Gacaca as strategic to the peace process in Africa. Never have we forgotten that we are brothers that are in the conflict within example Reverend Verse Pastor Genesis 13:1-8.
3. The Religious Market Place theory (building on our communalities like; market, football, schools, politics and so on) and Functionalists (if your religion claims peace let us see it practical) are highly recommended as a guide to promote tolerance and for religion to be used as a strategic guide to eradicate social injustice such as corruption which frustrates economic development. After all there will be no corruption in Africa if the people adhere strictly to the provisions of their faiths.
4. Again I strongly suggest the true practice of the godly values to stand out in desensitization and deliberation especially in the aspect of advocacy of social justice as in structural peace modalities.

References

Abdulla, A (2006). Principles of Islamic Conflict Intervention in West Africa by Best (ed). Spectrum Books Limited, Ibadan Nigeria.

Abubakar, A (2011). An Islamic Blueprint for Interreligious Peace Building in Northern Nigeria in religion and post Conflict Peace Building in Northern Nigeria by Best (ed). John Archers Publishers Limited Ibadan, Nigeria.

Benjamin, Junnang pokol (2018). "The Challenge of Christian Leadership in the 21st Century Nigeria: A Quest to Divorce the Church-State Marriage of Convenience and Rekindle the Prophetic Voice for Social Reconstruction". Magazine, Gindiri Theological Seminary, Jos Plateau State, Nigeria.

Best, S. (2011). Religion Conflict and Peace building: Conceptual and Theoretical Considerations In Religion and Post Conflict Peace Building in Northern Nigeria by Best (ed). John Archers Publishers Limited, Ibadan Nigeria.

Best, S. (2006). Conflict Analysis in Introduction to Peace Studies and Conflict Studies in Introduction to Peace and Conflict Studies in West africa by Best (ed). Spectrum Books Limited, Ibadan Nigeria.

Gamaliel, J. (2011). An Analysis of Religion under the 1999 Constitution and Prospects for Peace Building in nigeria in Religion and Post Conflict Peace Building in Northern Nigeria by Best (ed). John Archers Publishers Limited, Ibadan Nigeria.

Gerard Forde MA. A Journey Together; Muslims and Christian in Ireland: Building Mutual Respect, Understanding and Cooperation: A Response for Christian Muslim Dialogue. Cois Tine, 2013.

Gilchrist John. The Christian Witness to the Muslim. Benon RSA: Jesus to the Muslim, 1988.

Grim, B. (2014). Religious Freedom and Business Foundation, Religious Market Theory of Peace Yields Interfaith Harmony and Economic Growth Religious in Freedom and Business, Accessed: 15th October, 2015.

Gopin, M. (1997). Religion, Violence and Conflict Resolution: Peace and Change Vol. 22 Blackwell Publishing Limited

Gumut, V. (2006). Peace Education and Peer Mediation in Introduction to Peace and Conflict Studies in West Africa by Best (ed). Spectrum Books Limited, Ibadan Nigeria.

Gwamna, D. and Dayil, P. Religious Fundament in Northern Nigeria: Towards an Interpretation in Nigeria by Best (ed). John Archers Publishers Limited, Ibadan Nigeria, 20011.

Hansenclever, A. and Rittberger, V (2000). Does Religion Make a Difference? Theoretical Approaches to Impact of Faith on Political Conflict; Journal of International studies.

Huntingtom, S (1993). The Clash of Civilization: An Remaking of World Order. Simon Schuster. New York.

Imo, Cyril O Religion, Morality and Globalization. University of Jos Inaugural lectures. P.34, 2007.

Joseph Lengmang (2015). Lecture Notes on "Theories of Conflict and Conflict Resolution". Centre for Conflict Management and Peace Studies University of Jos, Nigeria.

Kendie, S and Guri, B. (2006). Indigenous Institutions, Governance and Development: Community Mobilization and Natural Resources Management in Ghana. Cape Coast, Ghana, Centre for Development Studies, University of Cape Coast Ghana.

Kwaku, O. and Rankopo (2010). Indigenous Conflict Resolution in Africa: Case of Ghana And Botswana. University of Botswana. Kukah, Hassan Matthew (1994). Religion Politics and Power in Northern Nigeria. SpectrumBooks Limited Ibadan, Nigeria.

Kukah, Hassan Matthew. Broken Truths: Nigeria's Elusive Quest for National Cohesion in a Convocation Lecture of 29th and 30th Convocation of the University of Jos, Nigeria On the Friday 22nd June, 2018.

Lamle, N. Elias (2015). An Introduction: Issues in Conflict and Peace Studies. University of Jos Press, Jos Nigeria.

Lamle, N. Elias (2015). " PCS 513 Religion, Conflict and Peace". CECOMPS University of Jos, Plateau State Nigeria.

Longkat, Daniel D. Lecture Note "Fundamentals of Peace Studies and Conflict Resolution" Gindiri Theological Seminary. Plateau State Nigeria 2017/ 2018.

Longkat, Daniel D. Lecture Note "Religion and Human Values" (GTS) Gindiri Theological Seminary. Plateau State Nigeria 2017/2018.

Luka Dinshak. Lecture notes *"Conflict Analysis and Management"*. Centre for Conflict Management and Peace Studies, University of Jos Nigeria, 2016. , *Theories of conflict, Conflict Analysis and management*. Taining of Trainers by TEKAN Peace Desk in Collaboration with Centre for Conflict Management and Peace Studies, University of Jos, Nigeria February, 2018.

Mangvwat, M (2011). Historicism and the Political Economy of Religious Crisis in Northern Nigeria by Best (ed). John Archers Publishers Limited. Ibadan Nigeria.

McCain, D and McCain, C (2011). A Christian Blueprint for Interreligious Peace Building in Northern Nigeria in Religion and Post Conflict Peace Building in Northern Nigeria by Best (ed). John Archers Publishers Limited, Ibadan Nigeria.

Moore, C.W. *The Mediation Process: Practical Strategies for Conflict.* San Francisco, California: Jossy-Bass Publishers. Pp .1 1996.

Nyampa Tizhe Kwabe. *Biblical Theology of Peace*: Training of Trainers by TEKAN Peace Desk in Collaboration with Centre for Conflict Management and peace Studies, University of Jos, Nigeria October, 2017.

Obadiah Samuel, Lecture Notes *"International Peace Keeping"*. Centre for Conflict Management and Peace Studies, University of Jos, Nigeria, 2015. *Understanding Conflict and Peace Studies.* Training of TrainersBy TEKAN Peace Desk in Collaboration with Centre for Conflict Mgt and Peace Studies, University of Jos, Nigeria February, 2018.

Oyeshola, Dokun. *Conflict and Context of Conflict Resolution.* Ile-Ife, Nigeria: Obafemi Awolowo University Press Limited. Pp 120. 2005

Ochonu, M (2014). Conflict between Muslims and Christians in Nigeria in Ground Project: The roots of Nigeria's Religious and Ethnic Conflict, Vanderbilt University, Nashville USA.

Pandang Yamsat. *Living our Christian Values and function even in difficult circumstance.* ACTS, Bukuru, Plateau State Nigeria. 2012.

Sunday, Bobai Agang (2017). No More Cheeks to Turn? Hippobooks, an imprint of ACTS, Langham Publications, WordAlive and Zondervan. Nairobi, Kenya.

Turaki, Yusuf (2012). Historical Roots of Crises and Conflict in Nigeria with Reference to Northern Nigeria and Kaduna state. Jos ECWA Theological Seminary, Nigeria.

Atlantablackstar.com. (Religious Tolerance, Ontario Canada www.religioustoleranceorg.

History and Heritage Travel in Africa: A Background of Joseph Kony and the Lord's Resistance Army. Peterbexterafrica.com. Accessed: 18th October 2015.

ARTICLE 5

Linkages Between Human Security and Peacebuilding in Post Conflict Environment

Simeon Oludele-Ajiboye

Research Fellow, Institute for Peace and Conflict Resolution, Abuja-Nigeria

Tel: +234 805 528 4977 E-mail: olusimeon@gmail.com

Abstract

A lot of concentration has been placed on the military or police to provide security, with huge expenses incurred on purchases of military hardware to maintain peace and security in Nigeria and elsewhere in Africa. Little attention has been given to other components of human security such as personal security, health security, economic security, environment security etc. This paper draws from the current debate on government's spending of $496million to buy 12 Super Tucano military aircraft to fight insecurity in Nigeria, in typical traditional security approach as against human (people-centred) security thinking. The paper contends that there is a linkage between human security and peace building and that the lack of, or inadequate attention to, one will jeopardise the other. Though the paper admits that there has been significant commitment by the state, international partners and donor agencies to address insecurity, especially in the Northeast of Nigeria, it posits that certain gaps demanding urgent attention are still identifiable. It proposes that for peace building activities to be successful, other elements of human security must be addressed. This necessity was evident in the Northeast where relief materials meant for internally displaced persons (IDPs) were sold by the victims and even stakeholders saddled with the responsibility of sharing them. This occurrence shows that certain aspects of human security have been neglected in the pursuit of peace building in the region. Failure to address this shortcoming will continue to pose threats to peace and security in Nigeria.

Key Words: Human Security, Peacebuilding and Conflict Environment

Introduction

Terrorism has become the biggest threat to Nigeria's internal security, and government's response to fight the threat has been inadequate. The failure of Nigerian state to respond adequately to threats has been attributed to improper use of the intelligence agencies; poor pro-active measures to nip the threats in the bud; and exclusive reliance on force in the management of the threats with little or no action taken to deal with the root causes of the challenges bordering on government issues (Thomas Imobighe, 2013). These factors have enabled insurgency in the Northeast to endure, impacted negatively on all aspects of human security and made post-conflict peace building difficult. The Nigerian government is heavily concentrated on how to win the terror war through huge military spending without giving priority to peace building activities which are critical to re-establishing human security battered by the insurgency in the region. This discourse focuses therefore on examining the linkage between peace building and human security.

Objectives of this Discourse

In this discourse, we will endeavour to achieve the following objectives:

1. Clarify the three concepts which are germane to this study, namely: human security, peace building and post-conflict society;
2. Explain the linkages between human security and peace building;
3. Examine the impacts of insurgency in the Northeast;
4. Suggest ways by which the country could effectively rebuild post-conflict Northeast.

Clarification of Concepts.

Human Security

Traditional security has been given much attention in the fight against insurgency in the Northeast while human security has been neglected. In order to have a clear understanding of what human security is, it is important to compare it with traditional security. Traditional security is state-centred, while human security is people-centred; traditional security protects and defends the state against external aggression, while human security protects persons against broader threats; traditional security sees the state as the sole actor, while human security involves regional and international organizations also; traditional security relies upon building up national power and military defence, while human security empowers people and societies to contribute to solution The 1994 UNDP Report introduces a new concept of human security, which emphasises people rather than territories; and development rather than arms (defence and security structures). According to the Commission on Human Security, human security "means protecting vital freedoms; protecting people from critical and pervasive threats and situations, building on their strengths and aspirations. It means creating (political, social, environmental, economic, military and cultural) systems that give people the building blocks of survival, dignity and livelihood." (www.humansecurity-chs.org, culled on 3 July 2018). It is clear that much emphasis has been placed on traditional security to fight insurgency in the Northeast, placing security above development, the state above the individual, and protection above empowerment.

Peace Building

Peace building refers to a set of activities designed and implemented to prevent and resolve violent conflicts, consolidate peace once violence has been reduced, and reconstruct after conflicts, with a view to avoiding a relapse into violent conflict. Peace building has been understood to include different levels of intervention as well as an overall strategy of human security pertaining to peace-related issues like relief and development, human rights and constitutional reform. The 'peace-building community' often refers to the human security dimension as an integral element of overall nation-building and state-building strategies. Most of the liberal theories of international relations maintain that for successful peace building, a minimally effective and legitimate state is necessary (Call, Charles T: 2007)

Post-conflict environment

The expression post-conflict environment/societies refer to countries in the aftermath of civil war. Such wars end as a result of negotiated peace accords or after the victory of one party. Such societies inherit a shattered political system, fragmented society and a devastated economy. Although Nigeria is not in a civil war, it has been at war against Boko Haram insurgents who once claimed part of the nation's territory and established its own government in the region. Post-conflict 'early recovery' has been used by many scholars to describe post-conflict societies in both policy and programmatic terms. For convenience and clarity, a post-conflict society in this discourse is a society that needs multifaceted intervention programmes after a war, in order to rebuild the war-torn communities and prevent a relapse into war. Development programmes such as rehabilitation of infrastructure, governance reforms, economic revitalization, demilitarization, security-sector reform, re-settlement of refugees, women & youth empowerment etc. are components of rebuilding post-conflict societies.

Methodology

The main methodology applied in carrying out this work was desk research involving a review of existing relevant literature and situation reports on the conflict situation in the Northeast, with a specific focus on terror attacks and their effects on human security and the linkage to peacebuilding in the region. Books, journals as well as on-line publications and other electronic sources of data were used. However, the limitation of this paper was the inability to carry out field trips to validate the findings from the literature and situation reports.

Effects of terror attacks on the Northeast

There is the temptation to justify the approval of the spending of $1bn military, considering the negative effects of Boko Haram violence on the Northeast. Everyone wants an end to Boko Haram violence because of its brutality and bad image it is giving Nigeria coupled with human and material losses. The first major attacks by Boko Haram took place in Borno and Bauchi States in June 2009, during the regime of the late President, Umaru Yar'dua. In a lecture delivered at the annual Murtala Mohammed Memorial, the Governor of Borno State, Kashim Shettima, gave grim statistics of deaths and material losses caused by Boko Haram. According to him,

> "insurgency has led to the deaths of almost 100,000 persons based on estimates by community leaders in the state over the years. Two million, one hundred and fourteen thousand (2, 114000) persons have become internally displaced as at December 2016, with 537,815 in separate camps; 158,201 are at official camps that consists (sic) of 6 centres with two transit camps at Muna and Customs House, both in Maiduguri. There are 379,614 IDPs at 15 satellite camps comprising Ngala, Monguno, Bama, Banki, Pulka, Gwoza, Sabon Gari, and other locations in the state. 73, 404 persons were forced to become refugees in neighbouring countries with Niger, having 1,402 and Cameroon, having 62,002" (Kashim Shettima: 2018).

The Governor stated further that, based on the post-insurgency Recovery and Peacebuilding Assessment (RPBA) on the Northeast, the report jointly validated by the World Bank, the European Union, the Government of Nigeria; Boko Haram had inflicted damages to the tune of $9billion on the region.

Impact on security. A threat to the security of a state is a threat to its existence, as it is rendered prostrate and vulnerable to violence and terrorism. Boko Haram terrorists attacked, sacked and burnt down many police stations, military barracks carting away weapons and killing many security personnel. The security situation was so bad at a time that no uniformed personnel could wear their uniforms in different parts of the region for the fear of being killed by the terrorists. It was reported that the entire Gwoza Mobile Police Unit in Borno was sacked and many officers were killed and abducted.

Moreover, terror attacks have caused great damage to the psychosocial well-being of the people of the region. Lamenting the trauma victims of terror go through, Ndibe noted thus:

> "Nigeria had been transformed into mini-Baghdad and Kabul; if you stand in a crowd in many towns in the northern part of the country, chances are that the man or woman standing next to you was, quite literally, a ticking explosive; in traffic, the car in front of, or behind you or to your right or left, may well be a vehicular bomb seconds away from detonating; in such a situation, life is nasty, brutish and potentially short; worse, such circumstances of extreme volatility and unpredictability mean that fear- a crippling brand of fear- is a constant companion to life" (Ndibe: 2012:55).

When people live in fear, it affects all aspects of human endeavours - political, economic, cultural and religious.

The effect of terrorist attacks on education cannot be overemphasised. The Northeast is the least region in school enrolment. According to the Nigerian education data survey released in 2010, school enrolment is 28% in Borno, Northeast Nigeria, the Boko Haram base; the continued attacks make it difficult for parents to let their children go to school; staff attendance has also dwindled; so far in 2012, 14 schools had been burnt down in Maiduguri, the capital of Borno State, forcing over 7000 children out of formal education and pushing down enrolment rates in an already ill-educated region (www.guardian.co.uk. 2012). Owing to Boko Haram attacks, lots of students were forced to abandon their education for fear of attack.

Terrorist attacks have also affected the economic development of the region. The economy of Northeast almost collapsed under the weight of insurgency activities. Maiduguri, which is well known for textiles, electronics, clothing and household items servicing neighbouring markets like Chad, Cameroon, Sudan and Central African Republic (CAR), came under the serious threats of Boko Haram. Insurgency in the region has thus contributed to the extant low level of capital flow via private investments. As observed by scholars, terror will cause investment to decrease and consumption decline in the long run.

Linkage of Human Security and Peace Building

According to UNDP Human Development Report 1994, "New Dimensions of Human Security", there are seven categories of human security. These are economic security, food security, health security, environmental security, personal security, community security, and political security.

Economic security includes insured basic income and employment, and access to social safety nets. The Northeast needs economic safety nets that will protect and promote livelihood through income-generating initiatives and social service programmes. It is understandable that government cannot provide employment for everybody, but it can create an enabling environment that stimulates economic activities by making available micro-finance loans. Small- and medium-scale enterprises are the drivers of the economy which can be encouraged through credit facilities with no or low interest rates. Peace-building efforts in these settings may also take the form of cooperative projects linking two or more communities in mutually beneficial undertakings that can not only contribute to economic and social development but also enhance the confidence that is so fundamental to peace (An Agenda for Peace: 1992).

Food security is simply physical and economic access to basic nutrition and food supply. When people do not have access to food or money to purchase food, it creates problems in the society. It has been widely reported that food as one of the relief materials supplied to the people in IDP camps are being sold by the camp officials as well as the beneficiaries themselves in order to get money. People in IDP camps cannot farm to produce their own food or make money from farm produce owing to insecurity in the states; hence, they resort to selling their rations in the camp for paltry sums. Sustainable peace can only be achieved when people have direct access to food, because as the saying goes, 'a hungry man is an angry man' The people in the Northeast have the rights to food as enshrined in international human rights law, but these rights have been grossly violated by the terrorists in the region.

Health security is more complex and covers many different issues such as access to safe water, living in a safe environment, access to health services, access to safe and affordable family planning and basic support during pregnancy and delivery, prevention of HIV/AIDS etc. Violence and conflict often lead to a collapse in the health care system and jeopardize the health security of those people caught in the vortex of conflict. The nexus between human security and peace building is appropriate health interventions that can increase the level of human security in conflict and post-conflict situations. Rehabilitating hospitals damaged by terrorists as well as building more hospitals; providing adequate quantity and quality drugs supplies; improving the capacity of health care personnel; and maintaining accessible, affordable and functional health care systems are parts of the peace-building process which will help the post-conflict recovery of the people of the Northeast.

Environmental security is straightforward and covers such issues as prevention of water pollution, prevention of air pollution, prevention of deforestation, prevention of natural hazards such as droughts, floods, cyclones, earthquakes etc. The Lake Chad Basin, which Nigeria is part of, has reduced about 90% in size in which about 23 million Nigerians are living around the basin coupled with desert encroachment, with significant impact on the social and economic well-being of the population in the region. This has brought competition for scarce resources, all of which have served as veritable instruments in the hands of the terrorists to unleash rampant violent conflict in the area.

Community security covers conservation of traditions and cultures, languages and commonly-held values. It also includes elimination and ethnic discrimination, prevention of ethnic conflicts, and protection of indigenous people. The tradition and culture of a man is his identity, so, as the insurgency erodes the culture and tradition of the citizenry, so is their identity eroded as a people. The people could no longer gather to observe and celebrate their cultures because of the fear of death through bomb blasts and other itinerant purveyors of disaster. Communal life no longer exists, as the citizens are perpetual soft targets of the terrorists

Personal security: A common approach to the peace-building process in a post-conflict society is the use of disarmament, demobilization and reintegration (DDR) programmes. These programmes are to reintegrate ex-combatants into civilian life and reunite communities. DDR programmes seek to create safe environments, enhance people's living standards through constructive means, and assist the community reconciliation process. Disarmament, as defined by the United Nations, is "the collection of small arms and light and heavy weapons within a conflict zone." Disarmament usually entails the use of incentives, often monetary, to encourage the giving up of weapons. At this stage in the programme, ex-combatants are typically given food aid, clothing shelter, medical attention, and are taught basic skills. (N. Hitchcock: 2004). Reintegration of ex-combatants through capacity building and self-employment is the hallmark of peace-building as was done in Sierra Leone. DDR is therefore a necessary component of peace building to ensure a stable post-conflict society. Many suspected Boko Haram insurgents that were arrested have been released, while many were reported de-radicalized. There has not been concrete DDR carried out for these de-radicalized Boko Haram members to prevent them from relapsing into violence. Ex-combatants need a channel through which they can exercise solidarity and affinity with their fellow community members.

Political security is concerned with the protection of political rights, human rights and the general political well-being of all the people. Specifically, it involves the protection of the people from state repression by ensuring the freedom of the press, freedom of speech, and freedom of voting. Violence in the Northeast has prevented the citizenry from exercising their franchise and has disrupted governance for a long time. The prolonged insecurity at a point even prevented local government administrations (LGAs) from functioning in some states in the region, thereby leaving the people at the local level without any semblance of governance. Peace building activities in the region is expected to gear towards addressing the root causes and drivers of violence and insecurity with a focus on human security rather than traditional security of huge spending on military hardware. Although, broader goal of military spending is to protect people generally, secure territory and national and community assets; in achieving these, human security should not be ignored or considered less important in the fight against insurgency in the North East. The nexus between human security and peace building therefore is to alleviate human insecurity and transform the social and political environment that encourages conflict situations.

Conclusion/Recommendations

This paper has strongly established the nexus between human security and peace building, positing that the human security is indeed the central focus of most peace building activities aimed at human development as well as sustainable and enduring peace. In order to prevent the vicious cycle of violence from re-emerging in the Northeast, measures to rebuild communities affected by violent conflict should be undertaken. These include:

Empowerment through education: As widely known, education in the Northeast is the most backward compared to other regions in the country, and it is made worse by the insurgent activities. Both formal and non-formal education systems should be encouraged, while the capacity of the teachers should further be rebuilt.

Rebuilding damaged basic infrastructures: Most communities affected by the insurgency have been completely destroyed. It is imperative to start the rebuilding of roads, hospitals, schools, markets and other infrastructure such as electricity, water pipes etc. that were damaged by the insurgents.

Good governance and accountability: The Northeast are the poorest region in Nigeria. There is the need for government to embrace key pillars of good governance, particularly accountability, and deal with corruption and nepotism. Government should also empower and revitalize local governments. Urgent and deliberate efforts are needed to make the state functional, responsive, responsible, transparent and accountable to the citizenry.

Agricultural development: The majority of the citizenry are peasant farmers who have been displaced from their farm land. Peace-building programmes that will facilitate the return of the farmers to their farm land should be embarked upon. This would ensure the empowerment of the people and improve the quality of their lives.

De-radicalization. The Nigerian Chief of Army Staff, on July 2018, handed over 183 arrested children from age 7-18 years associated with Boko Haram to Borno State Government and the United Nations (UN), for rehabilitation and reintegration, as reported by the National Television Authority (NTA). There should be proper rehabilitation and reintegration of these children who have been trained by the terrorists to detonate bombs, pull the trigger etc. These children should be De-radicalized.

Reference

Adetayo, Olalekan: "Boko Haram: Buhari approves release of $1bn for security equipment" Punch newspaper, 5 April 2018

Ashara Denis Uche: 2013, Trends, Effects and Panacea of Nigeria's terror ordeals. Center for Crisis Prevention and Peace Advocacy

"An Agenda for Peace: Preventive Diplomacy, Peacemaking and Peacekeeping: Report of the Secretary General Pursuant to the statement adopted by the Summit Meeting of the Security Council on 31 January 1992" Geneva, United Nations, 199 (A/47/277-S/24111)

Call, Charles T: 2007. Ending Wars, Building States, in: Call, Charles T. and Vanessa Hawkins Wyeth (eds), Building States to Build Peace, Lynne Rienner Publishers, Boulder, 2007.

Cropley and David Lewis Ed: (2015)" Nigeria drafts in foreign mercenaries to take on Boko Haram" Reuters.

"Global Terrorism Index 2015" Institute for Economies and Peace. November 2015. P. 41

Imobighe, T.A. & Eguavoen, A.N.T eds. 2006. Terrorism and Counter – Terrorism: An African perspective, Ibadan; Heinemann, pg. 16-18

Imobighe, T.A. Dimensions of threats and National Development Challenges in Nigeria; in "Internal Security Management in Nigeria" a study of Terror and Counter-Terrorism. Medusa Academic Publishers Limited, Kaduna-Nigeria. Pg. 16-17

Jack Moore: 2015, "Nigerian Military Enter Final Stages' of Boko Haram Offensive" Newsweek

N. Hitchcock, "Disarmament, Demobilisation & Reintegration: The Case of Angola," Conflict Trends, vol. 1, 2004, pp. 36-40.

Shetim Kashim, "Managing Boko Haram Crisis in Borno State, Experiences and Lessons for a Multiparty, Multi-ethnic and Multireligious Nigeria" www.premiumtimes.com. Sourced 18 June 2018

www.Guardian.co.uk. Retrieved 12 April 2012

www.humansecurity-chs.org/finalreport/Outlines/outline.html. Retrieved 3 July 2018

www.dailypost.ng. Retrieved 5 July 2018

The Implication of Organized Hatred. When Terrorists' Psyche is Culturally Bent.

BY
GABRIEL GYANG DUNG
gabrielgyangdung@gmail.com
08131650425

Abstract

Terrorists' calculation gets a nurtured environment from the organized hatred that keeps spreading like a wild fire as peace is gradually given way to violent conflicts which continue to dominate the fragile space in life. This work delves into the terrorists' psyche being culturally bent from the mirror angle of organized hatred. Leveraged by the qualitative means of analysis to bring the outcome to bare, the paper posits that the organized hatred is a direct innovation to socio-cultural ills such as violent attacks which destroy lives and properties across transnational borders in a way that the security structures find tough to contend. Hence, reversing the hardened psychology of miscreants and terrorists through attitudinal change, promoting love and harmony and again providing awareness from seminars and workshops to discourage any element of hatred within an in-group or out-group for peaceful coexistence and development.

Keywords: organized hatred, terrorists psyche and culturally bent

Introduction

The state of the mind is cardinally shaped, trained and leveraged by culture, society and heredity. From this end, terrorists have an orientational background that is bred in their way of life with a rich history of some certain tenets that are said to 'belief facts' which are passed down to younger generation, these they hold firm on to. The world is seemingly fragmented by blocs of hatred driven to violence and resulting in the destruction of lives and properties. All this happens in a predetermined realm of a hardened and conditioned state of the terrorists' psychology, groomed and handed over in a natural breeding milieu that is seen as a sustained morally just culture, which should and must continue within emerging contestational cultures. Terrorists and organized cultprits do not differ in their substance, but rather in their motives, Shelley and Picarelli (2001), and this shows a strong connection in their psychological hatred. The world is no doubt moving to somewhere with propelling drivers of coordinated hatred and terrorists' heinous justification in their very calculated act. The 2001 9/11 in USA reawakens the doubt to the safety of humankind, just managed to emerge from the long time cold war that puts the world on a high jump, asked so many questions relating to peaceful conditions but were buried unchecked and unanswered that seem to come into play at the present theatre of terrorism.

Williams (2009) contends that criminals do not border much about influencing or affecting public opinion, but to make money and get desires met, while the specific objectives of the terrorists' violence is keenly to distort the political structure. If the world now cannot properly check and answer the questions terrorists are asking, sooner or later, the world may beg terrorists operations to continue, just as a drug addict that withdrawing from abusing the drug, one would have to pay for it accordingly, as a withdrawal syndrome effect.

Different quarters of the world are faced with peculiar challenges of terrorism, though it has become a trans-national issue the world must contend with, yet, cultural curves in the terrorists psyche commune with organized hatred scattering the bearing of the old terrorism, thereby given way for the birth of new terrorism bringing the world in a new state of confusion, notwithstanding organized hatred and corruption appear to nest terrorists' activities in recent time. Corruption is one germane thing that has been figured out as a bane for growth and development which is seen as a nursery bed for social ill, Dung, Akaakohol and Akor (2014:310).

This paper raises some fundamental questions, seeking urgent answers to quell hardened and culturally curved mind of the terrorists in a polluted world of organized hatred. What is the implication of the organized hatred in culturally bent setting? What is the implication of the terrorists psyche in a culturally bent setting? To justify the position provoking for answers and to fill the gaps in this work and from the literatures in question, the paper will focus chiefly on how hatred and terrorists act partner for disaster, as such, will aim to examine the implication of the organized hatred in culturally bent setting, and also to examine the implication of the terrorists psyche in culturally bent setting.

THEORETICAL FRAMEWORK

Despotic evil reared in individuals and manifesting in technically organized selfish identities is an attitudinal culture that terrorists learned from preconceived hatred to preconceived explosion is what Ross exposed. The crux of this work revolves around the psycho-cultural conflict theory propounded by Ross in 1993. It opines that culturally induced conflicts present a kind of hatred-villient pictures including tangible and intangible materials that are deeply rooted in people concerning human actions, learned and sharpened their behavior for a very long term right from the process of growth and development in their lives or life cycle of a group for a particular motive such as violence, (Ross, 1993). From this point, the psycho-cultural conflict theorists submit that social disagreements that take much time before resolve, resulting in some groups being discriminated on the basis of their basic needs. When a violent conflict takes long duration before solution, the negative images stick in the human psyche and tend to formulate and situate the entire culture of life; this in turn grows to organized hatred with the ending in disaster of lives and resources.

In his exposition, as one of the leading exponents of realism, Morgenthau (1973:4) holds that the imperfection on the earth such as evil action, is rooted in the inherency in human nature and that by this reason, they tend to be selfish, individualistic and against the tenets of common good. This is clear from the above that, when human minds are debased and allowed to be bent by hatred, the generating action is a coordinated violence.

CONCEPTUAL CLARIFICATION

ORGANIZED HATRED

Hate is seen as an intense hostility and aversion always coming from fear, anger or perceived injury, or seen as an extreme dislike or antipathy (Webster Dictionary). Most of the war crimes and genocides committed against some races across the globe have been the bye-products of the organized hatred and some of these are: the (Holocaust) extermination of the German Jews during the Adolf Hitler's era, the Rwandan genocide of the 1994 among others. Raymond (1968) holds that there is no gain saying that to over generalize the modern peace movements, this shows that terrorism is influenced by hatred which also attaches to secrete admiration for ideological and political adversaries. And again, going forward on this menace called hatred, the ideological forgeries means that so rarely is hatred obvious and straight in nature but rather acts in pretence for evil.

TERRORISTS PSYCHE

The notion that what act can be qualified as terrorism or terrorists operation appears to be uneasy question (Cooper, 2001; Moghaddam, & Marsella, 2004). Even though (Moghaddam & Marsella, 2004) recommend certain points to all terrorists' acts to include: violence, deliberate imposition of fear against the civilians with the aim of inducing changes in people's statusquo especially in political and socio-cultural positions.

Moreover in defining terrorists psyche, it cannot be devoid of political connotation as it implies a state of political stances to determine the legitimacy or absence of legitimacy of rebellious action for mere destructive agenda to instill fear, maim or kill. The way and manner terrorism and terrorists' mental state are fashioned and labeled show different political and socio-cultural implications resulting in the interaction between two or more communities whose conflict may breed terrorism

(Kruglanski, Crenshaw, Post and Victoroff, 2007). Suffice it to say that conflict which is generated and not properly engaged, will bounce a huge deficit on the lives and properties.

CULTURALLY BENT

Every people have their unique way and manner in which certain features, traits, belief, customs including orientation, showcased across the globe, but the way and manner these attributes are played around sometimes construe and constitute a severe challenge to other people and gradually spread across borders. Often times, some people combine ethnicity and grievances which mobilize structural difference, straight-jacketed psyche, hatred and violence (Ndonye, social media). Differences in cultural backgrounds over the periods have been a source of disunity rather than a cohesive tool for contributing unique attributes on board. There are basically two types of persuasion: direct and indirect, the direct concerns to mass media exponentiality which widens hatred that drives to violence of ethnic groups. On the other hand the indirect persuasion sales out hatred and process behavior towards implementing violence, Petrova and Yanagizawa-Drott (2016). Terrorism and hatred of certain belief are the deadliest and sustaining.

ORGANIZED HATRED IN A CULTURALLY BENT SETTING

People all over the world have recognized that despite their geographical situation with peculiar identities and cultures, yet, they still acknowledge that something binds the human race and can still live together in peace. Technically organized hatred like stereotype, xenophobia, discrimination, racism and other hateful contents are bred in a biased cultural setting. This may seem to be insignificant from where it starts, however in reality, it is a wild fire in action learning from the examples of the Apartheid in South Africa, the Rwandan genocide, the Nigerian civil war (Biafran war) among other lessons witnessed or learned across the globe. A good "hit lists" fashioning out physical attacks on the opponents of organized hate groups or clear minorities are showcased ("Redwatch" wibesite in the Czech Republic, Poland, Russia and UK and antiabortion "hit lists" of abortion clinic doctors in a number of countries).

When people believe that they have been badly treated, particularly by a group viewed to be the enemy, the climax is always dehumanizing those viewed as "them". A minute group or the target of hatred or even the target of the projected and dislike features of the self becomes less human in that capacity, in such instances, violence pushed against "them" because "they" are not regarded as humans. In all sincerity, almost everything can be compromised to justify not only organized hatred, but as well, hatred at the individual's level. Many people you sight in life that are in a happy mood could be the result of discomfort situation others are found, Dung (2014:4). This shows the level to which organized hatred works and how extremely reverse, hatred can go against genuine happiness among people.

Cultural and ideologically fanatism are salient instruments people use to justify the act of dehumanizing others seen as obstacles to achieving their ideal aspect in life. A hardened culturally bent Osama Bin Ladin in his justification of the attack launched on the world trade centre in USA,

2001 9/11 that resulted in the deaths of about three thousand people armless, by saying that he wished to enthrone a system of life on earth in accordance with God's will. It is pertinent to note that Osama Bin Ladin is only one out of the many radical people or groups whose hatred is culturally conceived and nurtured for launch, having a long historical negative images concerning life.

TERRORISTS PSYCHE IN CULTURALLY BENT SETTING

More than ever, it is becoming more worrisome and difficult to determine the action of terrorists in a fast dynamic world. Culture and mindset are veritable tools terrorists hinge for sustainable operation. Brown (1996) analyzed cultural or perceptual factors like other factors to have the propensity and tendency in causing violent conflict. Identity structure where membership is recognized for premeditated acts of violence is readily bred in mind before execution. It is not individual's mental state, but rather groups, organizational and social psychology with a keen emphasis on collective identity which avails the most strongest lens in understanding the terrorists' psychology and behavior, Post (2005).

The early theorists that emanated from psychology came from clinical psychology and psychiatry. The reason of these propositions is to elicit substances from which terrorists' personality may manifest sooner or later in life. One fundamental assertion puts forward by Post (2005) holds that terrorists are mentally sound at the level of not being clinically psychotic as some may view. Furthermore, they are neither depressed, seriously emotional scattered nor stupid extremists. Terrorist groups and organized criminals first examine and screen out any emotionally unstable individuals in the group for security reason in their operations. This means that they have a careful and well plans and even deploys techniques ahead of ordinary people's expectations, no wonder, the public often gets surprised and confused by the time that they unleash their dreaded acts.

THE DANGER OF TERRORISTS FREEDOM IN A CHARGED VOLATILE ATMOSPHERE

One critical adjective that the world is heart-beated in more than any time in a given human race is 'security' and the business of security must trail on sound security structure. Human or basic rights are different from the fundamental rights, although freedom as a fundamental right is a legal value that is universally inclined which every human being needs and is entitled to. (UN Charter Arti. 55©) spells that human rights are all over, that is they are inherent in all human beings which are interdependent and indivisible. Some of these international human rights and treaties include: the convention against torture and other cruel, evil and inhumane treatment or punishment, with all these rising rights, conventions and protocols across the globe for the protection of human and fundamental rights and freedom, in turn give the terrorists and miscreants a soft ride and capitalize on to unleash their heinous operations. The constitution of the Federal Republic of Nigeria is clear as to the limit to exercise such rights so as not to infringe on other people's rights, the Constitution of Nigeria as amended (1999: sect. 45(1)). By the time everybody is given a free hand by the security architecture of the government to operate at volition, the hoodlums always take advantage of the porous security in place for mayhem.

ETHNOCENTRIC REVIVAL, A HYBRID OF EVIL EXPANSION

Realistic group conflict theory seeks to explain the bias-based of in-groups with symbolic threat which tends to be stronger predictors of practical behavior towards out-group. Intergroup threat theories provide a framework for intergroup biases and aggression, Stephan and Stephan (2000). Socio-cultural aggrandizement has given a new line of thoughts that the current generation has to grapple with so much that an individual or group is not only looking at others as inferior, but as well, evil. Parker and Janoff-Bulman (2003) submit that the intergroup threat occurs when one group's interests threaten another group's goals and wellbeing.

Ethnic superiority interwoven with racism and the two conflate in such a manner that nothing good is seen or expected from an out-group. Societies of the world are faced with stiff challenges bedeviling features and patterns that keep the human material life in the state of harmony. Drawing from the examples the heightening rivalry, threats, and tensions of all sorts across the global frontline from one ethnic coloration to a group's dangerous plans and these very ill-factors are promoted on a daily basis, which degenerate into violence. Terrorism of today began as a lesser threat and ills of socio-cultural tenets and ideologies of an in-group growing at a high speed and the implication now is what the world has to contend with as terrorism.

TERRORISM AND HATRED, A SIMPLE TWIST OF DISASTER

Attacks and violence are increasingly becoming asymmetrical leaving scores hard to bear with the dawn of current challenges of terrorism and hatred that are no longer conventional in nature and magnitude. Prior to 9/11 2001 trade centre bomb detonation in USA, good number of terrorists acts were depending on the conventional means of explosives. An act of assault or harm directed against a person or group of people by another person or group thereby putting the wellbeing of the victim(s) on a deficit is said to be a violent conflict, Lamle and Dung (still in a press) .The sudden change in this modus operandi stems from the singular hatred and terrorists acts leveraged by new opportunities, population explosion amidst scarce resources, innovation and technological enhancement today. Several twirling patterns of calculated evils are accounting for, for structural and systemic failures in life, whose implication is the widening effect at the moment. Kiras in Baylis and Smith (2001) would say that technology together with the patterns linked with globalization do inspire terrorism to accelerate and change from just a regional menace to that of global. It is heart-warming to keep in view, how challenges take advantage on conflict situations to write a new dreaded face and how poignantly that could seem in the feature.

A combination of the organized ill-factors support one another to feature pools of problem subjecting people to deliberate socio-economic, cultural and political frustration especially in a weak security architectural climes of the world. The weak domains of the world are much vulnerable to violent conflict with end result in collapsed and then failed state and that this may not stop there within the shores and boundaries of the very state as the case with terrorists, crossing borders.

THE ORGANIZED HATRED VIS-À-VIS TERRORISTS MISCHIEF AND THE IMPLICATION TO PEACEFUL COEXISTENCE

Movements and ideologies aim at enhancing negative conflicts are becoming the order of the day in many angles of the world, and this is clear from the ongoing attacks ranging from the individual(s) to group(s) and to the general public. Many societies are suddenly awakened by the application of threat and violence which drive the world easy and tend to pin to the wall.

Peace holds a paramount social intention that looks to positively change the current human issues by transforming the social structures and lines of thoughts that produce it. Hatred is the first tool that terrorists harbor and mobilize which has the ability of triggering violence against a particular group or the general public. United States of America's Federal Bureau of Investigation (FBI) submits that hate group's initial purpose is to enhance animosity, hostility and malice against persons who are members of a race, creed or ethnic national origin that differs from the members of the organization, US FBI, (2015). The collaboration between the organized hatred and terrorists' conspiracy has a salient threat to peaceful coexistence. (US FBI, 2015) holds that the larger an extremist group is and the longer it has existed, the more readily the group is to engage in violence. Peace is a virtue that comes from within the mind of a person. Gbgm-umc.org (2013), in his swift exposition, Joseph E. Agne holds that hate motivated violence is the outcome of successes of the civil rights movement and furthermore, the Ku Klux Klan (KKK) has resurfaced for the emergence of new hate groups. Destruction of lives and properties will appear to be the ultimate reign which decimates any peaceful coexistence.

CONCLUSION AND RECOMMENDATION

The increasing tempo of violent conflicts has given a new birth to terrorists' activities that clearly originate from cumulative organized hatred hovering in and around the formal and informal structures of the societies. The humans mind that is spoiled by hatred subsequently degenerates into a coordinated violence is a visible expansion of evil.

The work submits that the culture of impunity rared in the realm of both natural and artificial organized hatred invents the socio-cultural ills that hunt, attack and destroy lives and properties in human societies on the globe and the implication of these vices is the increasing speed of terrorism in asymmetric manner.

This paper exposes the ills of the organized hatred and the cultured terrorists psyche as the leading drivers in the destruction of lives and other resources. From this standpoint, it suggests that attitudinal change is possible from the lines of exploring equity and justice, emphasizing common love, tolerance together with sincere mandate for human development by both public and private authorities for the overall peace in human life.

References

Brown M. E. (1969). The International Dimension of Conflict. Cambridge Massachussets: The MIT Press.

Constitution of Nigeria (1999). Constitution of the Federal Republic of Nigeria 1999.

Cooper, H. H. A. (2001). Terrorism: the problem of definition revisited. American Behavioral Scientist, (44)6, 881-893.

Dung, G. G. (2014). The Blissful Road. A Play. Gold Ink Company, Katsina-Ala, Benue State. ISBN: 978-978-52273-3-8.

Dung, G. G., Akaakohol, B. M. And Akor, J. C. (2014). Katsina-Ala Multidisciplinary Journal. Vol. 2 No. 1 2014. ISSN: 2141-0992.

Gbgm-umc.org (2013). "The church's Response to Hate Group Violence". Gbgm-umc.org Achieved from the original on 2012-02-24. Retrieved 2013-09-14.

Kiras, J. D. (2001) in Balyis, J. and Smith, S. (eds.). Terrorism and Globalization. The Globalization of Work Politics. An introduction to IR Chapter 21, Oxford, Oxford University Press.

Kruglanski, A. W. Crenshaw, M., Post, J. M. & Victoroff, J. (2007). What should this fight be called? Metaphors of counter terrorism and their implications. Psychological science in the public interest, 8(3), 97-133.

Lamle, E. N. and Dung, G. G. (still in the press). Changing The Narratives Of Violent Conflicts: Issues Of Unemployment And Poverty Among The Youths In Plateau State.

Moghaddam, F. M. &Marsella, A. J. (eds.). (2004) Understanding Terrorism, Psychological Roots, Consequences and Interventions. Washington DC:American Psychological Association.

Mogenthau, H. (1973) Politics Among Nations: the struggle for power and peace, 5th edition. New York: Alfred, A. Knopt.

Ndonye, M. M. (social media). Ethnic hatred and peace journalism: case of twitter and facebook use in kenya.

Parker, M. T.; Janoff-Bulman, R. (2013) "Lessons from mortality-based social identity: the power of outgroup "hate", not just ingroup "love". Social justice research. 26:81-96.

Petrova, M. and Yanagizawa-Drott, D. (2016). Media persuasion, Ethnic Hatred and Mass Violence: a brief overview of recent research advances.

Post, J. M. (2005). When hatred is bred in the bone: psycho-cultural foundations of contemporary terrorism. Political psychology, 26(4), 615-636.

Raymond, A. (1968) Democracy and Totalitarianism. Trans. Valence Ionescu (London: Weidenfeld and Nicolson, 1968.

"Redwatch", website in the Czech Republic, Poland, Russia and UK and anti abortion "hit lists" of abortion clinic doctors in a number of countries.

Ross, M. (1993). The management of conflict: interpretations and interests in comparative perspectives. New Haven: Yale University Press.

Shelly, L. and Picarelli (2001) "Methods not Motives: implications of the convergence of international organized crime and terrorism".

Stephan, W. G.; Stephan, C. W. (2000). "An integrated theory of prejudice". Reducing prejudice and discrimination: the Claremont symposium on applied social psychology: 23-45.

United Nations Charter, Art. 55©, The Universal Declaration of Human Rights, Art. 2 and the Vienna Declaration and plan of action.

US FBI (1999). "Hate Crime Data Collection Guidelines", uniform crime reporting: summary reporting system: national incident-based reporting system, US department of justice: Federal Bureau of Investigation, Criminal Justice Information Services Division, Revised October 1999.

US FBI (2015). Frequently Asked Questions. Federal Bureau of Investigation. Retrieved may 30th 2015.

Williams, P. (2009). "strategy for a new world: combating terrorism and transnational organized crime" in Balyis, J. (eds.) chapter 9.

A Discourse on the Role of Language in Logic: Snytax and Semantics[1]

Barrister Buduka Isaac Oyagiri
Babcock University, Ilisan Remo, Ogun State
Email: graceforbuduka@yahoo.com. Tel: 234 803 5918 860

Abstract

Logic is both the science and art of reasoning. As a science it discovers the rules of reasoning and as an art, it applies the rules of reasoning to correctly state or deny a claim or proposition. In fact, the central concern of logic is argument. Argument makes use of a great deal of language to express its main claims or to oppose one established by the opponent. It is therefore important that these propositions have structure or form and should clearly expressed the meanings intended by the arguer and seen that the listener got the same meaning. This was one of the cardinal role of language in logic. Logic is interested in the relationship symbols, texts, signs etc have with the objective or subjective constructions ascribed to them in real life. The paper was completed by desk based research. This afforded the writer opportunity to see many secondary sources for appreciating the role of language in logic. The paper achieved the depiction of the trio relationship between language and logic, syntax and logic and semantics and logic and therefore insisted that language played major role in logic in both the formal sentence construction, how it works, and the ascription of meaning to the sentence. The paper in its concluding remarks, posited that the essence of language in logic and those of syntax and semantics are akin to make argumentation pure, intelligent and meaningful. It is by means of syntax and semantics that logic achieves this.

Keywords: Language, Logic, Syntax, Semantics

---

[1] Oyagiri, Buduka Isaac Lecturer II, Babcock University School of Law and Security Studies Iperu Remo, Ogun State.

1 INTRODUCTION

The term 'logic' is coined from the Greek word *logos,* which has variously been interpreted as sentence, discourse, reason, rule, and ratio. It has been referred to as a science which deals with the principles and criteria of validity, inference and demonstration. It is also the formal principle of reasoning[2].

Logic is one of the traditional sub-disciplines of Philosophy and one of the seven traditional Liberal Arts[3]. There are many good reasons to study Logic[4]; it helps to separate correct from incorrect reasoning, know how to use language and ideas precisely and thus, enhance understanding, take rational decisions when faced with alternatives, to detect and avoid fallacies[5], give insight into linguistics[6].

Logic is the science that deals with necessary laws or forms of thoughts and principles of any branch of knowledge

Logic lies at the foundation of mathematics, where it allows us to provide a clear and rigorous account of mathematical proof. It also plays a central role in philosophy, where we use it to help reason as clearly and as rigorously as possible about hard questions about ourselves, about knowledge, reality, truth, and beauty, and about right, wrong, good and bad. It also lies at the foundation of Computer science: a computer is a logic machine. In addition, a mind is, at least in part, a logic machine too, so logic lies at the foundation of Cognitive Science and Philosophy of mind. It also, more importantly, for the purpose of this work, lies at the foundation of Linguistics, providing the tools we use for thinking about linguistic structure (syntax) and linguistic meaning (semantics).

2 WHAT IS SEMANTICS?

To appreciate the meaning of semantics one needs to first inquire to know what is linguistics? Because only by so doing can we find the present discourse useful as semantics and syntax are domiciled in language.

Linguistics is the science of language (and its structure) including phonetics, phonology, morphology, syntax, semantics, pragmatics and historical linguistics.[7] While, Semantics as a sub-division of Linguistics is interested in the study of meaning. In fact, Semantics is the study of the relationship between words and meanings.[8] i.e. it is the study of the meanings of elements, words, etc.

Semantics is simply the study of meanings. In a much broader spectrum, however, it may be defined as the historical and psychological study, and the classification of changes in the denotation

---

[2] Jossy C. Achilike (1999) *Fundamentals of Logic,(2ⁿᵈ ed., Ben-El Books Publishers)p.6; see also* Chimemzie Omeonu A,et. Al., (2013) *Introduction to Logic & Critical Thinking,* (Natural Prints Ltd.), Pp.28-29 & 52-53.

[3] alongside arithmetic, geometry, astronomy, music, grammar, logic and rhetoric.

[4] Philosophy 112, What is Logic, Retrieved 25 February, 2018 from < https://www.davidsanson.com>

[5] Chimemzie Omeonu A,et. Al., (2013) *Introduction to Logic & Critical Thinking,* (Natural Prints Ltd.), p. 52.

[6] Jossy C. Achilike p.6.

[7] Thesaurus.com, Retrieved 25 January, 2019 from <https://www.dictionary.com/browse/linguistics>.

[8] The Columbia Encyclopedia 6ᵗʰ Ed. Retrieved 23 June, 2018 from https://www.encyclopedia.com/literature-and-arts/language-linguistics-and-literary-terms/language-and-linguistics/semantics.

of words or forms viewed as factors in linguistic development.[9] The Online dictionary defines Semantics as the branch of Linguistics and Logic concerned with meaning. The two main areas are Logical Semantics, which is concerned with matters such as sense and reference and presupposition and implication, and Lexical Semantics, which is concerned with the analysis of word meanings and relations between them.

Logical semantics is a branch of Logic that deals with the study of meaning and sense of concepts, propositions, and of their formal analogues – the interpretations of expressions. The first and foremost task of Logical semantics is to define precisely, the concept of "meaning", "sense" and "interpretation" and accordingly, the concepts of "truth", "definability", "impressibility".

Semantic problems arise because of the difference between the content and extension of concepts and between the meaning and truth-value of propositions.

Semantics is therefore interested in the following:

a. How meanings work in language
b. The way in which words are put together to create a meaning
c. The relationship between the words i.e the synonyms, antonyms etc.
d. The relationship between sentences and fifth point ambiguity is what makes us see in this logical sense why it is important to first understand semantics before one can properly understand logic
e. Ambiguity: A sentence becomes ambiguous when it has two or more meanings. A sentence can be ambiguous in two different ways:
    i.   Lexical Ambiguity: A sentence is lexically ambiguous when it can have two or more possible meanings due to polysemous (words that have two or more related meanings) or homophonous (a single word which has two or more different meanings) words.[10]

         An example of an instance where a statement is lexically ambiguous is "serial Killers appeal to the judge" in this sense it could mean that the Judge likes serial killers or that the serial killers seek the mercy of the Judge.

         From our earlier classes, we have come to understand that there are errors in logical reasoning and they are called "fallacies" Fallacies are broadly divided into informal and formal fallacies. The above example shows language users in informal fallacy commit these types of error due to carelessness or when the statements are ambiguous. The example afore mentioned falls under the fallacies of ambiguity.

    ii. Structural ambiguity: A sentence is structurally ambiguous if it can have two or more possible meanings due to the words it contains being able to be combined in different ways, which create different meanings[11].

         An example of such an instance is: "The mother beat her daughter because she was drunk". It is easy to see that this statement is ambiguous because it is not clear whether

---

[9] Merriam Webster dictionary, Semantics
[10] 'What is Semantics', https://sites.google.com/a/Sheffield.ar.uk/aal2013/branches/semantics/what-is-semantics accessed 23 February, 2018
[11] Ibid p.1 – 4.

the woman beat her daughter for getting drunk or whether the woman beat her daughter because she herself was drunk. In any case, it could be either both or any one sense above is the correct meaning of the proposition.

Semantics and Logic are therefore intertwined in such a case as it is very difficult if not impossible for logicians to be able to present a sound and valid argument that is void of fallacies if one does not initially understand the meaning and relationship between words which is what semantics hopes to achieve. The link between logic and semantics is such that one cannot boast to have understood logic and its concepts if he does not first understand semantics and its concepts.

3 THE TRIAD RELATIONSHIP BETWEEN SYNTAX, SEMANTICS AND LOGIC

Here, the relationship is gotten from semiotics, which is the study, theory, or science of signs. With the use of an example of ordinary language (like English) as the system of signs (letters, punctuations, numerals, words, expressions etc). Logic and computer programming languages and instructions sets are formed (not ordinarily) sign systems but the same concepts and principles apply in all these cases.[12]

Semantics refers to the relations signs have to the things they stand for or represent in some way; in other words, providing the lexicon and truth theory determining semiotic meaning and truth

It is a branch of linguistics and logic is concerned with the meaning of words and concepts representative of real order in that we are dealing with things, not as they are in themselves, but as they are in thoughts, in the world of idea before being expressed concretely. The definition of an object is concerned with the nature of the theory.

RELATIONSHIP BETWEEN LOGIC AND SEMANTICS

Semantics is the branch of linguistics and logic is concerned with the meaning of words and concepts representative of the real order. Here we are dealing with things, not as they are in themselves but as they are in thought. The object of logic is to consider the entities as objects of thought in the conceptual order; i.e in the mind.

In logic, the semantics of logic is the study of semantics or interpretations of formal and natural languages usually trying to capture the pre- theoretic notion of entailment.

In Linguistics, Semantics hashes out the relationship between words and phrases and their meanings. Semantics, as a branch of linguistics and logic is concerned with the meaning of words and concepts representative of the real order. Here, semantics plays a role in reasoning, arguing and thinking.

For instance, according to Terence Parr, "a language is a set of valid sentences. Furthermore, the validity of a sentence can be broken down into two things: Syntax and Semantics. The term syntax refers to grammatical structure, whereas, the term semantics refers to the meaning of the vocabulary

---

[12] Terry Rankin (1998) Semiotic Representation (2nd edition) Wells- House Publishing Limited, p. 18 =semiotics, Retrieved 10 January, 2019

symbols arranged with that structure. Grammatical (syntactically valid) does not imply sensible (semantically valid), however". For example, the grammatical sentence "Men cry technologically" is grammatically correct (containing the subject, verb and adverb) in English, but makes no sense.[13]

We can also consider statements below:

1. she likes tofu and
   He likes ice cream
2. she likes ice cream and
   He likes tofu
3. she likes ice cream and
   He likes ice cream

In all these sentences, let us put them in a form "and" (x only). This pattern is the logical form we see in all three sentences. These sentences do not mean the same thing but once we apply a little bit of meaning to that logic (x and y), we get three sentences and we can determine if they are right or wrong. For example

1. she likes tofu and
   He likes ice cream $\quad$ x - t $^\wedge$ y - i
2. she likes ice cream and
   He likes tofu $\quad$ x- i $^\wedge$ y - t
3. she likes ice cream and
   He likes ice cream $\quad$ x - i $^\wedge$ y – i

In the above, the key for symbolization are she = x, he = y, tofu = t and ice- cream = i

4 MODERN APPROACHES TO SEMANTICS

The main modern approaches to semantics for formal languages are the following:

i. Model-theoretic semantics is the archetype of Alfred Tarski's semantic theory of truth, based on his T-schema, and is one of the founding concepts of model theory. This is the most widespread approach, and is based on the idea that the meaning of the various parts of the propositions are given by the possible ways we can give a recursively specified group of interpretation functions from them to some predefined mathematical domains: an interpretation of first-order predicate logic is given by a mapping from terms to a universe of individuals, and a mapping from propositions to the truth values "true" and "false". Model-theoretic semantics provides the foundations for an approach to the theory of meaning known as Truth-conditional semantics, which was pioneered by Donald Davidson. Kripke semantics introduces innovations, but is broadly in the Tarskian mold.

---

[13] Terence Parr

ii. Proof-theoretic semantics associates the meaning of propositions with the roles that they can play in inferences. Gerhard Gentzen, Dag Prawitz and Michael Dummett are generally seen as the founders of this approach; it is heavily influenced by Ludwig Wittgenstein's later philosophy, especially his aphorism "meaning is use".

iii. Truth-value semantics (also commonly referred to as substitutional quantification) was advocated by Ruth Barcan Marcus for modal logics in the early 1960s and later championed by Dunn, Belnap, and Leblanc for standard first-order logic. James Garson has given some results in the areas of adequacy for intensional logics outfitted with such a semantics. The truth conditions for quantified formulas are given purely in terms of truth with no appeal to domains whatsoever (and hence its name truth-value semantics).

iv. Game-theoretical semantics has made resurgence lately mainly due to Jaakko Hintikka for logics of (finite) partially ordered quantification which were originally investigated by Leon Henkin, who studied Henkin quantifiers.

v. Probabilistic semantics originated from H. Field and has been shown equivalent to and a natural generalization of truth-value semantics. Like truth-value semantics, it is also non-referential in nature.

5 THE RELATIONSHIP BETWEEN LOGIC AND SYNTAX

Logic has been intertwined with the study of language and meaning since its inception, and such nexus persist in present day research in linguistic theory (formal semantics) and cognitive psychology (for example, studies of human reasoning). However, few studies in cognitive neuroscience have addressed logic dimensions of sentence-level language processing, and none have directly compared these aspects of processing with syntax and lexical/conceptual-semantics

In logic, syntax is anything that has to do with formal languages without regard to any interpretation or meaning given to them. Syntax is concerned with the rules used for constructing, or transforming the symbols and words of a language.

Syntax is usually concerned with the grammatical rules governing the composition of texts in a formal language that constitute the well-formed formulas of a formal system.

The word 'syntax' has a rich ancient Greek history and may mean coordination, to arrange or put in order. It also means the grammatical structure of words and phrases to create coherent sentences.[14]

While studying languages and how they function, we must study syntax and sentence constructions. Studying syntax is relevant to a lot of subject areas in linguistics. We must study syntax to understand how learners acquire their language, how they start constructing sentences and what stage do they learn the tactic syntactic rules of the language. It is also good to study syntax so we can understand how bilingual and multilingual speakers are able to construct their sentences despite having different structures for different languages. The sentence structure is not the same in English as it is in Ekpeye language among Ekpeye people of Rivers State. In short, syntax varies

---

[14] Writing explained, 'what is Syntax? Definition, Examples of English Syntax' (2018) retrieved from https://writingexplained.org/grammar-dictionary/syntax 13 March, 2019.

widely in different languages, although it aids language speakers to construct sentences properly and putting phrases and words in their correct positions.[15]

5.1 WHY IS SYNTAX STUDIED?

It is our nature as human beings to study things and to gain an understanding of how they work. So while studying how they work, you must study syntax and sentence construction.

Again studying syntax is important to a lot of subject areas in linguistics. We must study to understand how children acquire their language, how they start making up sentences and what stage do they learn the tacit syntactic rules of the language. It's also good to study syntax as it helps us understand how bilingual and multilingual speakers are able to construct their sentences despite having various structures for various languages.[16]

Further, the study of syntax gives us many answers which are necessary for understanding how languages work, as well as being the doorway to future research and theories on all aspects of linguistics[17].

We also syntax to develop set rules and constraints on the language. These can be called parameters. These parameters limit what we can and don't do in a language, helping us establish an effective and working communicative system. Some linguistics believe that all languages have the same parameters. This is called universal grammar, and was a theory developed by Chomsky in the 1960s. From these ideas of linguistic parameters, we can learn, use and teach the correct way to make sentences basically, so we can all understand each other[18].

5.2 SYNTATIC ENTITIES

Syntatic entities includes symbols and formal language

A symbol is an idea, abstraction or concept, tokens of which may be marks or a configuration of marks which form a particular pattern.

A symbol or string of symbols may comprise a well formed formula if the formulation is consistent with the rules of the language. Symbols of a formal language must be capable of being specified without any reference to any interpretation of them. While, formal language may refer to formally defined set of strings as considered in theory of automata and formal language[19]. It is formally defined languages that are similar to natural languages (vernacular), in the sense that both are used to convey meaning through representatives of that meaning. We have to convey meaning to others, or even ourselves (when we take notes)

---

[15] Richard Norquist, Syntax Defintion and Discussion of English Syntax Retrieved from hhttp://www.thoughtco.com/syntax-grammer-1692182

[16] Copi Irving (1979) *Introduction to Logic*(5th ed., New York Macmillian Press)p. 35-36

[17] Jossy C. Achilike (1999) *Fundamentals of Logic,*(2nd ed., Ben-El Books Publishers)p.8.

[18] Okafor F.U.,(2005) An Outline for the Use of Snytax and Semantics in Logic (1st ed., Wilstone Publishing House) p. 15.

[19] Popper Karl (1982) *The Logic of Scientific Discovery,* (1st ed., Hutchinson Publishing House) p.34.

6 FUNCTIONS OF LANGUAGE IN LOGIC

The formal patterns of correct reasoning can all be conveyed through ordinary language, but then, so can other things too. The basic functions are generally noted. There is perhaps nothing more subtle than language and nothing as different as it is. It is a social tool for reference, instruction, and communication and may be verbal or non-verbal.

There are three distinct functions of language and they are:

a. The informative use of language: this is communication employed for the purpose of asserting propositions or presenting arguments. It involves an effort to communicate some content. For example[20], If I tell a child that; "the 1st of October is a public holiday" or write to you that "logic is the study of correct reasoning" or even just a note/memo to myself, I am using language informatively. It presumes that which is being communicated is absolutely true. Informative function affirms or denies propositions, as in science, or the statement of a fact. It is also used to describe the world of reason about it, for instance, whether a state of affairs has occurred or not or what might have led to it.

   Also, these sentences have a truth value; that is, the sentences are either true or false, recognizing of course, that we might not know what truth value is, hence, they are important for logic

b. The expressive use of language: this is communication that gives vent to feelings, attitudes, or emotions. For example[21],

   If I yell "ouch" or say "Monday mornings are dreary", I'm using language with expression.

   Although, such uses don't convey any information. They serve an important function in everyday life since how we feel sometimes matters as much as or more than what we hold to be true

   Poetry and literature are among the best examples but much of, if not all, of ordinary language discourse is the expression of emotions, feelings or attitude.

   Expressive discourse is best regarded as neither true nor false. E.g., Shakespeare's King Lear's Lament, "Rapeness is all" or Dicken's It was best of time, it was worst of times; it was the age of wisdom, it was the age of foolishness". Even so, the "logic" of fictional statement is an interesting area of inquiry.

c. Directive use of language: This is communication that aims to bring about or forestall the performance of some action. When I say "shut the door" or "read the textbook", or memo myself, I am using language directly. The point in any case is to make someone perform a particular action. This is a significant linguistic function, but like the expressive use, it doesn't always relate logically to the truth of our beliefs.

---

[20] R.G. Lipsey (1969) *An Introduction to Positive Communication; Use of Language,* (1st ed., Methuen and Co. Limited), p. 63.

[21] Chimemzie Omeonu A, et.al., (n. 4), p. 58.

Without doubt, identifying just these three functions is an over simplification, but an awareness of these functions is a good introduction to the complexity of language. Language users and logicians have found these very useful.

As seen above, the directive function is most commonly found in command and requests. Directive language is not normally considered true or false, even though various logics of command have been developed.

It is rare for discourse just to serve only one function even in a scientific treatise, discursive (logical) clarity is required but at the same time, ease of depression often demands some presentation of attitudes or feeling otherwise the work might come off as dull[22].

Most ordinary kinds of discourse is mixed. Consider the example; suppose you want your listeners to contribute to the issue of Ebola spread, there are several approaches to it:

i.   Explain the recent breakthrough in the scientists understanding of the disease (informative) and then ask for a contribution (directive)

ii. Make a moving appeal (expressive) and then ask for a contribution (directive)

iii. Command it (directive)

iv. Explain the good results (informative) make a moving appeal (expressive) and then ask (directive)

v.   Generally speaking, step 3 (specifically stating that which is desired as outcome) is the least effective means, usually, just making a moving appeal is most effective for the general population explaining the recent research is the most effective for an educate audience.

vi. The ceremonial: also known as ritual language probably something quite different from simply mixing the expressive and directive language functions because performative aspects are included as well. E.g., Dearly beloved, we are gathered here together to witness the holy matrimony of...[23]

vii. Performative utterances: language which performs the action it reports, for example, "I do" in a marriage ceremony and use of performative verbs such as "accept", "apologize", "congratulate", and "promise". These words denote an action which is performed by using the verb in the first person- nothing more needs to be done to accomplish the action

viii. Phatic language: "elevator talk" and street corner conversations accomplishing a social task, note the subtle transition from vocal behavior to body language from saying for example, "hi" or "how are you?" to a nod or a wave of hand.

In all these 'performatory' exercises as in oaths incantations, passwords and rituals, there must be no change in exact words otherwise it will not valid or sufficient compliance. For instance before assuming any public office in Nigeria, one must swear the oath of allegiance in the exact words as provided in the Constitution thus:

---

[22] Douglas Saluer, *An Essay on the Relationship between Semantics and Logic*, Retrieved 19 July, 2018 from http://logicmanual.philosopy.ox.ac/uk/vorlessung/logic2.pdf.

[23] Jossy C. Achilike (n. 13)p.8.

I, … … … … … … … …. do solemnly swear/affirm that I will be faithful and bear true allegiance to the Federal Republic of Nigeria and that I will preserve, protect and defend the Constitution of the Federal Republic of Nigeria. So help me God.[24]

Therefore, in its performatory sense, language is like any other gesture or symbol. Austin estimates that there are over a thousand performative verbs in English linguistics.[25]

Language also functions to tell a story, to disclaim, to hypnotize, to play a part, to imagine, to soothe, to ask, to deceive, to demonstrate one's feelings and in endless other ways. Therefore, when it comes to talking about what language actually does, one needs to be aware that language actually functions in variety of ways each of which may have slightly different rules of behaviour. [26]

Language will help users and logicians as basic liberal tool for education, expand understanding, it limits barrier and misconceptions, it improves our knowledge base, builds up vocabulary and interpretative skills. Other uses of language includes enhancing users listening skills and ability to memorise ideas, concepts things etc. it is equally useful for analysis and problem solving while positively altering attitudes of users[27]. Effective language use should remove or prejudices and fears of insecurity because we understand what is being said.

---

[24] Seventh Schedule of the 1999 Constitution of the Federal Republic of Nigeria (as amended)

[25] J L Austin Stanford Encyclopedia of Philosophy, *Retrieved 20 March, 2019 from* https://plato.stanford.edu>austine-jl

[26] Philosophy 103: Introduction to Logic, *Common Forms and Functions of Language, Retrieved 10 March, 2019 from <www.philosophy.lander.edu>logic>form_lang.com>.*

[27] Leonardo De Valoes, 'Importance of Language – Why Learning a Second Language is Important' 14 March, 2019 from https://www.trinitydc/continuing-education/2014/2/26/importance-of-language-why-learning-a-second-language-is-important/

Some strategic security challenges for Africa in the twenty-first century (part 1)

By
Dr. Peter Onime (BSc., MSc., MBA, DM)
413 Marengo Avenue 102, Forest Part, IL 60130, USA
peteronime@yahoo.com

Abstract

Africa accounts for about 16% of the world's population while occupying 20% of the global landmass. Despite these facts, Africa is responsible for a minuscule 2-3% of the global economic activity. This paper discusses some of the challenges that Africa is expected to face in the twenty-first century. These range from climate change to diminished emigration opportunities. To cope with these oncoming issues, this article proposes that Africa enacts some structural reforms around becoming an outward-looking society while enhancing its analytical capabilities, augmenting transparency, and ensuring a commitment to the rule of law.

1. Introduction

Global security has become topical amongst academics and policymakers. The diminishing global security alarm has been raised on various aspects of security such as the rising global levels of indebtedness (Lachman, 2016) and the impending resource scarcity (United Nations, 2019). Even global trade has become a security flashpoint. Barely a week now passes without some geopolitical security issue.

This was not always the case. There was a time around the turn of the last century where there was broad consensus in many parts of the world about the benefits of globalization. While globalization has been around since ancient times, the pace of globalization had quickened in the immediate years before the beginning of the twenty-first century (Rizescu, 2013).

Nevertheless, the long-standing consensus amongst the policymakers in both the western world and other parts of the globe has frayed as to whether the benefits of deepening economic interdependence and ever closer integration between countries outweigh the potential downsides of globalization (Wright, 2013).

Some of the serious doubts about globalization that have been raised in the western world (which was the erstwhile bastions of globalization) had been foreseen. In a prescient article, Wright (2013) predicted the loosening of the global consensus partly because the risks associated with globalization would cause some states to reassess the whole globalization project. That prediction has been proven right. With this in mind, the question for both the general population in Africa and their policymakers is what the changing landscape of globalization and the associated risks mean for the continent.

This article is the first in a two-part series and identifies some strategic considerations that Africa should engage in as it seeks to re-organize itself in the next thirty years. This work then proposes some structural reforms to mitigate the identified issues. A future follow-on article (part two) will discuss some specific changes that Africa should implement in order to better secure its future.

1.1. Some Basics about Africa

The continent of Africa has an area of 30 million square kilometers and ranks as the second-largest continent in the world. Using this measure, Africa accounts for about 20% of the world's land area (World Atlas, 2019). About 1.1 billion people live in Africa out of an estimated global population of just over 7 billion people. This again makes Africa the second largest continent by population with about 16% of the world's population (World Atlas, 2019).

While the size and population of the continent are about 15-20% of the global total, the economic performance of Africa is unaccomplished. Indeed, Africa accounts for just over 2% of the global economy when using the measure of nominal GDP (World Population Review, 2019). Therefore, Africa has underperformed economically relative to its size and population.

There is a wide variety of publications that have researched and analyzed the anemic economic performance of Africa (Onime, 2000; United Nations, 2018). Rather than focus on the economic contribution alone, this work pursues the supposition that Africa should consider a rationale for instituting economic improvement as a means of strengthening the security of the continent. In a world where the economic direction now appears to be heading towards building fortress economies (Washington Post, 2019), it is doubly important for Africa to view economic performance as part of a broader security understanding.

2. Some Security Issues Facing Africa

2.1. Climate Change

Probably the greatest challenge facing humanity as a whole is the projected impact of unchecked global climate temperature rise in the next 50 – 100 years (United Nations, 2019). The current predictions envisage a global effect of climate change. Africa with its large landmass and relatively long coastline will likely be very much affected.

Even a small increase in global sea and ocean levels could have a significant negative effect on the coastal dwellings in Africa. Rising sea levels are not the only postulated impact of global warming. Other potential effects of climate change include increased desertification, degradation of arable land, challenges in maintaining sustainable land, and reduced food security (United Nations, 2019).

2.2. Other Security Issues that Africa Faces

There are also a variety of other security issues that could impact Africa. Onime (2000) predicted seven other issues that could be expected to affect Africa in the course of the twenty-first century.

While the century is still young, a review of these predictions that compares them to the trends of the first two decades of the new century is in order.

2.2.1. Changing Nature of the Nation-State

The first predicted issue was the acceleration of the changing nature of the nation-state. This prediction referred to the fact that many nation-states would individually possess fewer tools to impact global events. This relative lack of control over external events often leads to a higher level of frustration amongst the citizens.

The relative powerlessness to control external events remains a valid issue for many African countries who have very few mechanisms to affect the geopolitical and economic forces that constantly buffet the countries in Africa.

2.2.2. Challenge of Inequality

The second prediction centered on a trend that societies in the twenty-first century would gravitate towards increasing egalitarianism. While the jury is still out as to if this is a fully accurate prediction, the early trend appears to be in the direction of increasing equality. Even if the global trend was counter to this direction, a move towards more equality represents a good policy for Africa.

This prediction of increasing egalitarianism is not intended to revisit the pros and cons of capitalism, socialism, and other organizing human economic models. The central premise of this prediction is justified by recent evidence that suggests that higher levels of inequality represent a security risk for human civilizations (Nuwer, 2017).

2.2.3. Democratic Participation

The third prediction was that African leaders could expect to come under additional pressure to increase democratic participation in their countries and also enact substantive democratic reforms. This pressure currently exists and will remain as long as African citizens have more visibility into the quality of life in other nations. This comparison of the quality of life in Africa against other places then serves to elevate the demand for improved governance.

2.2.4. Pragmatism versus Ideology

Fourthly, the author (Onime, 2000) foresaw that the twenty-first century would be less ideological than the twentieth century. In this instance, this prediction does not appear to be fully correct. There are signs of movement towards authoritarianism in some western countries and some of the other democracies. Nevertheless, in the wider world, there does seem to be a trend towards a focus on pragmatism. This trend of more pragmatism also appears to be the case in Africa.

2.2.5. Continuous Learning

The fifth issue identified for Africa was that in order to be successful in the twenty-first century, countries and organizations needed to move to more continuous forms of learning. This method of learning includes conceptual thinking, commitment to excellence, systematic learning, shared goals, and group learning (Senge, 2006). Continuous learning and improvement have become critical in this century. Therefore, this challenge remains relevant to Africa.

2.2.6. Self-Reliance

Another prediction for Africa in the twenty-first century was that Africa could expect less and less help from the wealthier parts of the world. This appears to be the case for the first two decades of the new century. There are a variety of reasons for this state of affairs. Some of the wealthier countries have their own economic challenges. Other countries are experiencing donor fatigue together. These two factors contribute to an increasing mindset of building a protective economic (and sometimes literal) fortresses around the country (Washington Post, 2019; Wright, 2013)

2.2.7. Less Immigration

The seventh and final issue that was predicted in this new century was that Africa would face a reduced acceptance of poor immigrants from Africa. These economically downtrodden immigrants have become a flashpoint in some parts of the world such as the European Union countries and the United States of America.

Paradoxically, the higher emphasis that wealthier countries now place highly gifted and qualified immigrants from Africa will put further increase the pressure on Africa. Consequently, the already elevated (and largely unsustainable) rate of brain drain from Africa to the rest of the world has the potential to even increase.

Individually, each of these challenges is difficult. Collectively, these predictions represent a clear and present danger to the future well-being of Africa. Therefore, the time for urgent action is now.

3. Structural Security Steps Africa can and Should Take

Each of the previously stated challenges ranging from climate change to brain drain represents a pressing security risk for Africa. In order to successfully face these issues, Africa would have to enact some structural changes. These are discussed in the remainder of this chapter below.

3.1. Develop an Outward-Looking Focus

There is now general acceptance in literature that the flow of talent has become global (D'Costa, 2008; Verburg, Bosch-Sijtsema, & Vartiainen, 2013). This idea should not be surprising. The corollary of this fact is that the quality of people now represents the greatest asset that a country or organization possesses (Stanciu & Tinca, 2013).

This global talent also brings with them the acquired knowledge deriving from lifelong learning (Senge, 2006). This nexus of high-quality talent anchored by continuous learning often drives creativity and innovation. Creativity is the ability to find new practices or processes (Kerzner, 2013) and innovation translates any creative ideas into solving specific societal problems (Kerzner, 2013; Kumar, 2012).

It is now understood that countries (like individuals) require creativity and innovation to retain a competitive edge (Shafie, Siti-Nabiha, & Tan, 2014). Therefore, Africa needs to structure itself in such a way as to attract the best global talent (in addition to growing top-class talent at home). This outward focus is critical for Africa.

This global outlook does not detract from the need for Africa to strive for self-sufficiency. Self-sufficiency in key areas such as basic agriculture, infrastructure, and general socio-economic institutions requires an outward look in order to obtain the benefits of the best of breed global knowledge and ideas. This is where developing and acquiring the best talent will pay off for Africa even as it strives for full self-sufficiency.

3.2. Develop Critical Analysis Skills

Critical analysis skills underpin various aspects of creativity and innovation. It is difficult to create new ideas or build innovative products without first critically reviewing or analyzing the status quo. Consequently, critical analysis often produces some form of criticism.

This criticism can be manifested in various ways such as pointing out the shortcomings of an existing idea, critiquing people, or even criticizing leaders. This analytical process should be encouraged while recognizing that any questioning of the existing state of affairs is integral to the critical analysis process (Onime, 2000).

Consequently, Africa should adopt the ethos of questioning which underpins critical analysis. This openness to considering other ideas has been shown to be indispensable for creativity and innovation (Bogdanowicz, 2014; Girdauskiene, 2013; McManus, 2015; Nwibere, 2013).

Critical questioning should be encouraged at every level of society ranging from children to authority figures, and even leadership. Questioning should not be seen as disrespectful. For Africa to reap the benefits of an outward-looking society, it should cultivate a questioning mentality that accepts criticisms.

3.3. Improved Transparency

An open culture is also necessary for the long-term success of societies (Bogdanowicz, 2014; Girdauskiene, 2013; McManus, 2015; Nwibere, 2013; Onime, 2000). Transparency allows countries to ask difficult questions, accept unpleasant answers, and undertake any painful remedial actions. Critical analysis without transparency ultimately erodes people's trust especially when difficult changes are required. The lack of transparency also detracts from the goal of driving innovative change.

While full transparency may not always be possible in every sphere of life, the goal for Africa is to strive for as much transparency as appropriate. In practice, transparency involves Africans accepting any unpleasant results of analysis without being defensive. For example, it will behoove Africans to accept the unhappy analytical result of the dire state of affairs on the continent without the need to justify the status quo with mitigating excuses. Certainly, the first step towards solving any difficult issue is to accept the results of the problem analysis.

3.4. Improved Focus on the Rule of Law

So far, the proposed structural changes in Africa include a) developing an outward focus, b) enhancing critical analysis, and c) improving transparency. To underpin the drive for transparency, Africans must be confident that societal laws and regulations will be applied fairly, equitably, and transparently.

Consequently, the continent should commit itself to support the rule of law. For the laws to be respected, there should be robust mechanisms to obtain buy-in from the general populace and stakeholders even before laws are promulgated.

This is where democracy does have some advantages if correctly designed and applied. The overriding aim of a democratic system should be to do the greatest good for the greatest number of people. In aligning to this goal, one innovation that Africans could contribute to human governance is to **design** the **next level** of democratic governance that a) does the greatest good for the greatest number of people, b) resists capture by the elite or the very wealthy, and c) is very accountable. The system would thus strive for equal justice for all; perceived and real; de facto and de jure.

Nevertheless, while a well-designed democratic system for Africa is not a panacea to all of Africa's problems, it represents a necessary starting point to addressing the considerable challenges that the continent faces (Onime, 2000).

4. Conclusions

Some of the security challenges facing Africa in the twenty-first century include climate change, the diminishing capacity of many nation-states to confront geopolitical forces, societal inequality, large democratic deficits, preference of ideology over pragmatism, lack of continuous learning, poor self-reliance, and reduced emigration opportunities for Africans. These items constitute a formidable and possibly existential threat to Africa.

This work proposes that Africa starts by enacting some structural reforms. These changes include: developing an outward-looking focus, building up critical analytical skills, improved transparency, and a relentless focus on the rule of law.

These proposals will enable Africa to mitigate the impacts of climate change, build capacity to confront the geopolitical forces affect the continent, reduce societal inequality, minimize the present democratic deficit, elevate pragmatism over ideology, institute continuous learning, become self-reliant, and reduced the pressures for African emigration. These changes should enable Africa to achieve its true potential. A future article will propose some more specific reforms over and above these structural changes.

References

Bogdanowicz, M. (2014). Organizational culture as a source of competitive advantage – Case study of a telecommunication company in Poland. [Article]. *Kultura Organizacyjna Jako Źródło Przewagi Konkurencyjnej – Studium Przypadku Firmy Telekomunikacyjnej W Polsce, 13*(3), 53-66. (Accession No. 109188154)

D'Costa, A. P. (2008). The barbarians are here. *Asian Population Studies, 4*(3), 311.

Girdauskiene, L. (2013). The key factors for creativity implementation and knowledge creation in an organization: The structural approach. *Economics & Management, 18*(1), 176-182. doi:10.5755/j01.em.18.1.4305

Kerzner, H. R. (2013). *Project management: A systems approach to planning, scheduling, and controlling* [VitalSource Bookshelf Online](11th ed.).

Kumar, V. (2012). *101 design methods: A structured approach for driving innovation in your organization* [VitalSource Bookshelf Online](1st ed.).

Lachman, D. (2016). A False Sense of Global Security? *International Economy, 30*(2), 56-79.

McManus, J. (2015). Creating transformation in project management: A point of view. [Article]. *Management Services, 59*(1), 20-24. (Accession No. 101883658)

Nuwer, R. (2017). How Western Civilisation Could Collapse. Retrieved from http://www.bbc.com/future/story/20170418-how-western-civilisation-could-collapse

Nwibere, B. M. (2013). The influence of corporate culture on managerial leadership style: The Nigerian experience. [Article]. *International Journal of Business & Public Administration, 10*(2), 166-187. (Accession No. 91955995)

Onime, P. I. I. (2000). *A vision for Africa*. UK: Minerva.

Rizescu, M. (2013). Globalization and its consequences in international economic organizations. [Article]. *Managerial Challenges of the Contemporary Society, *(6), 81-84. (Accession No. 95589860)

Senge, P. M. (2006). The learning organization. In W. E. Natemeyer & P. Hersey (Eds.), *Classics of organizational behavior.* (Fourth ed., pp. 587-591). Long Grove, IL: Waveland Press, Inc.

Shafie, S. B., Siti-Nabiha, A. K., & Tan, C. L. (2014). Organizational culture, transformational leadership and product innovation: A conceptual review. [Article]. *International Journal of Organizational Innovation, 7*, 30-43. (Accession No. 102561439)

Stanciu, V., & Tinca, A. (2013). ERP solutions between success and failure. [Article]. *Accounting & Management Information Systems / Contabilitate si Informatica de Gestiune, 12*(4), 626-649. (Accession No. 94433877)

United Nations. (2018). Human development reports. Retrieved from http://hdr.undp.org

United Nations. (2019). Climate change and land. Retrieved from https://www.un.org/en/climatechange/reports.shtml

Verburg, R. M., Bosch-Sijtsema, P., & Vartiainen, M. (2013). Getting it done: Critical success factors for project managers in virtual work settings. *International Journal of Project Management, 31*(1), 68-79. doi:10.1016/j.ijproman.2012.04.005

Washington Post. (2019). We're moving toward a world of fortress economies. Retrieved from https://www.washingtonpost.com/politics/2019/08/24/trumps-order-us-companies-leave-china-shows-that-world-economy-is-being-transformed/?noredirect=on

World Atlas. (2019). Map And Details Of All 7 Continents. Retrieved from https://www.worldatlas.com/aatlas/infopage/contnent.htm

World Population Review. (2019). GDP Ranked by Country 2019. Retrieved from http://worldpopulationreview.com/countries/countries-by-gdp/

Wright, T. (2013). Sifting through Interdependence. *The Washington Quarterly, 36*(4), 7-23. doi:10.1080/0163660X.2013.861706

About the Author

International Journal of security and Security Studies (IJoSSS) is an open access, online/print-on-demand, and peer-reviewed Journal on Security and Strategic Studies published and supported by Infinity Systems Consult International in Affiliation with the Department of Security and Strategic Studies, Institute of Governance and Development Studies Nasarawa State University Keffi, Nasarawa State Nigeria. International Journal of security and Security Studies (IJoSSS) presents National, Regional and International perspectives on Security, Human Security Strategy issues and studies from historical and reality assessments, by disseminating graduate research and all-purpose research work internationally, IJoSSS seeks to facilitate students, scholars and professional acquisition of knowledge from alternative viewpoints allowing them to further develop critical thinking, problem-solving, and global competencies required to lead in a complex world. International Journal of Security and Security Studies (IJoSSS) presents National, Regional and International perspectives on Security, Human Security Strategy issues and studies from historical and reality assessments by disseminating graduate research and all-purpose research work internationally. IJoSSS seeks to facilitate students, scholars and professional acquisition of knowledge from alternative viewpoints allowing them to further develop critical thinking, problem-solving, and global competencies required to lead in a complex world. IJoSSS: knowledge from alternative viewpoints, develop critical thinking, problem-solving, and global competencies required to lead in a complex world.